Knowing Where You're Going:™
New York City

navigate the neighborhoods like a native

James C. Schmitt

"And because no matter who you are, if you believe in yourself and your dream, New York will always be the place for you."

-*Michael Bloomberg*

With special thanks to . . .

My wife Donna, who spent many long hours doing the layout design, marketing and promotion. She also logged many miles on foot, both above and below ground, exploring every neighborhood, park and subway station in Manhattan, as we researched this book.

Patti Middleton, who did the painstakingly tedious job of proofreading all the maps and text.

My family and friends, who encouraged, advised and shared their own knowledge of New York City.

This book is dedicated to the memory of my grandfather, Alfred F. Bowden, who realized the American dream in the great city of New York. I have many fond memories of him teaching and quizzing me on my knowledge of Manhattan. I believe he knew that the first step towards making it in the Big Apple was simply "knowing where you're going".

For Gary . . . .

table of contents

table of contents

Get "In The Know"!

Welcome to Knowing Where You're Going™: New York City!
This book is your ultimate NYC exploration tool, whether
you are visiting from overseas or just over the river. We'll
take you neighborhood by neighborhood, and give you the
essential information needed for a safe, stress-free, and fun
adventure in the greatest city in the world.

New York City is a huge place. You could spend a lifetime
exploring its streets and discovering its secrets. To the
uninitiated, the city seems like one giant conglomeration
of streets and buildings. In reality, it's comprised of many
smaller neighborhoods, each one with its own special per-
sonality and flavor. In most cases businesses, shopping, and
restaurants are clustered together on a particular street or
streets, just like any town. Looking at these maps, you'll be
able to see at a glance the layout of every neighborhood in
Manhattan. No more wondering if you are missing something right around the next corner. No more wandering
several extra blocks before you realize there isn't anything
more you want to see. This guide is designed to be a trea-
sure map of sorts. While no map can possibly inform you of
everything you might possibly find, these maps will show
you in no uncertain terms, where to look. The joy of New
York City is in the discovery. You'll see things you've never
seen before, guaranteed.

The maps in this book throw aside traditional or "official"
neighborhood boundaries, and provide a simple snapshot
of where the action is. At a glance, you'll see the scope and
layout of the various business districts - and what you will
find there.

Streets worth exploring are outlined with heavy black lines.
These are major neighborhood thoroughfares, where you'll
find businesses, shopping, restaurants, and attractions. More

importantly, these streets are safe and filled with people going about their business.

I've designated streets that are home to an abundance of retail stores as shopping districts by highlighting them in purple. Information regarding what types of stores you will find along a particular stretch can be found on the adjoining text pages.

Restaurants in New York come and go, but where they are located tends to stay the same for decades. I've highlighted these restaurant districts in yellow on the maps.

MAP SYMBOLS

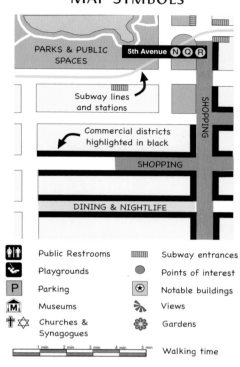

The city has so many culinary choices, it can be an adventure just reading all the menus and finding the perfect atmosphere and food to fit the moment.

So come on...push those boundaries, step out of your comfort zone! A few blocks or a few subway stops away is a whole different world filled with wonderful things to see and do. Read on and explore new frontiers with confidence. With this book to guide you, you'll "know where you're going"!

KEY MAP

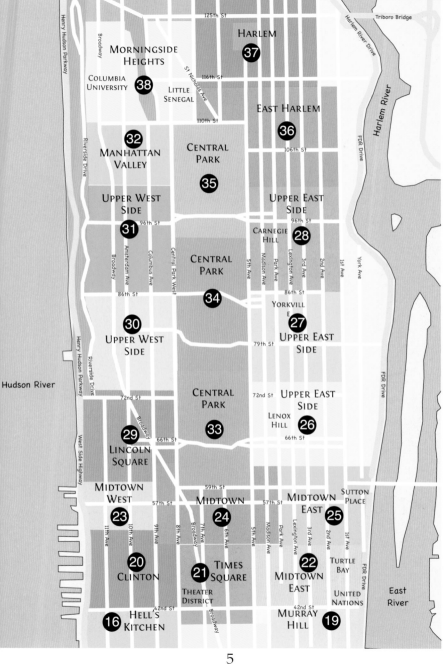

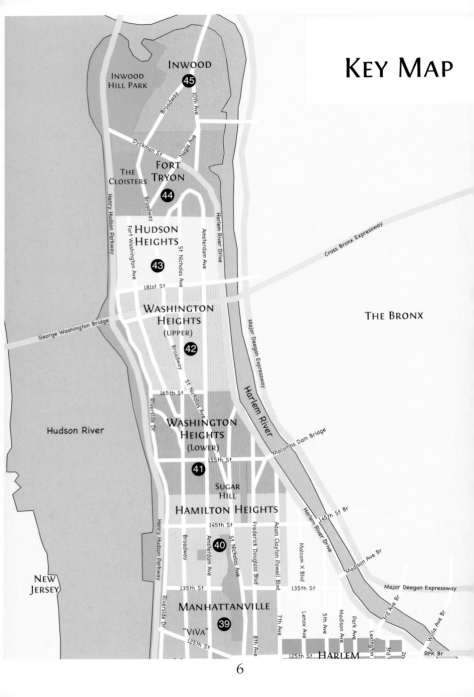

KEY MAP

Inwood
Inwood Hill Park
45

Broadway
10th Ave

Dyckman St
Nagle Ave

THE CLOISTERS
FORT TRYON
44

Broadway

HUDSON HEIGHTS
St. Nicholas Ave
Amsterdam Ave
Harlem River Drive
43

Fort Washington Ave
Henry Hudson Parkway

181st St

Cross Bronx Expressway

WASHINGTON HEIGHTS (UPPER)
42

Broadway

THE BRONX

George Washington Bridge

Major Deegan Expressway

Harlem River

165th St
St. Nicholas Ave

Riverside Dr

WASHINGTON HEIGHTS (LOWER)
41

Hudson River

155th St

Macombs Dam Bridge

SUGAR HILL

HAMILTON HEIGHTS

145th St
Broadway
Amsterdam Ave
40
St. Nicholas Ave
Frederick Douglass Blvd
Adam Clayton Powell Blvd
Malcom X Blvd
Harlem River Drive
145th St Br

135th St
135th St
Madison Ave Br

Riverside Dr
Henry Hudson Parkway

NEW JERSEY

MANHATTANVILLE
39
"ViVa"
125th St

7th Ave
Lenox Ave
5th Ave
Madison Ave
Park Ave
Lexington
3rd
2nd
3rd Ave Br
Willis Ave Br
RFK Br
Major Deegan Expressway

8th Ave
125th St HARLEM

6

TEXT SYMBOLS

 Points of interest

 Museums

 Neighborhood Events

 Parks and Public Spaces

 Dining

 Shopping

 Nightlife

 Transportation/Getting around

LOWER MANHATTAN MAP 1

Lower Manhattan is the oldest and most historic part of New York City. The original Dutch settlement was founded in 1625 and was known as New Amsterdam. When control of the colony shifted to England in 1665, the city was renamed New York.

 Wall Street

In the early 1600s, Wall Street was the northern border of the city. The street was named for the stockade wall that once stood here as a defense against Indian raids. Originally a slave market, Wall Street soon evolved into a locale where traders would meet to buy and sell securities. An agreement signed in 1792 by twenty-four stockbrockers led to the creation of the New York Stock Exchange. Today the NYSE is the largest stock exchange in the world, and Wall Street is synonymous with American business, finance and investing. Over a hundred billions dollars changes hands here every day.

 Trinity Church

Originally built in 1698, Trinity Church is by far the oldest church in New York. Rebuilt three times, the present structure was the tallest building in the city until 1890. The churchyard is open to the public and is the burial site of many famous historic figures.

New York Stock Exchange

 Federal Hall

George Washington was inaugurated as the first president of the United State on the steps of Federal Hall in 1789.

 Governors Island

A five-minute ferry ride away, the 172-acre Governors Island sits in the channel between Manhattan and Brooklyn. A military outpost since colonial times, the island was declared a national monument in 2001. Visitors can take walking tours and rent bicycles. Several fairs and festivals take place during the summer months. Ferries depart from the historic Battery Maritime Building.

Statue of Liberty

Created by Frederic Auguste Bartholdi and constructed in 1886, Lady Liberty was a gift from the French to the American people. Ferries leave from the tip of Battery Park every 30 minutes. Once reaching Liberty Island, one can visit the museum and observation deck.

 Staten Island Ferry

One of the most scenic boat trips in the world - and it's free! The five-mile journey to the borough of Staten Island takes about 25 minutes and offers breathtaking views of the New York skyline, the Statue Of Liberty, and Ellis Island. Ferries run around the clock.

 Museum of Jewish Heritage

Also known as the Holocaust Museum, the museum was created to be a celebration of Jewish life and culture, as well as a memorial to those who perished in the Holocaust.

 Ellis Island

The U.S. point of entry for over 12 million immigrants between 1892 and 1954. Now the site of the Immigration Museum, visitors can see where their ancestors first set foot on U.S. soil and find their names on the Immigrant Wall Of Honor - the largest wall of names in the world.

Skyscraper Museum

Dedicated to the history, technology, design, and construction of high rise buildings.

 Museum of the American Indian

Dedicated to the history and culture of the native peoples of North America.

 New York Police Museum

Preserves the history of the New York Police Department. Features educational programs and exhibits.

 Museum of American Finance

Dedicated to the history and documentation of American financial history. Exhibits historic artifacts related to the financial markets, money, and banking.

 Hudson & East River Esplanades

Beautiful views of New York Harbor can be had from these waterfront walkways. The Hudson River side is home to several waterfront parks and restaurants, while the East River esplanade serves as a scenic route to the South Street Seaport (see map 3).

Battery Park

Located at the southernmost tip of Manhattan, Battery Park offers unparalleled views of New York Harbor. Created largely from landfill, the park expanded and surrounded Castle Clinton, which was originally built as an artillery defense post 300 feet offshore. It is presently a national monument and museum, and houses the ticket office for ferries to the Statue of Liberty and Ellis Island. The park contains many monuments, notably "The Sphere", a sculpture that once stood in the plaza at the World Trade Center and miraculously survived the attacks of 9/11. It was re-erected in Battery Park as a memorial.

Battery Park

Hudson River Greenway

The Hudson River Greenway is a popular multi-use path that runs along the Hudson waterfront for just over 12 miles. It begins on the west side of Battery Park and connects all of the parks along Manhattan's west side.

 Bowling Green

Bowling Green is the oldest park in New York City. At the northern tip of the park stands the famous "Charging Bull" sculpture. Anatomically correct, rubbing a certain area of the bull is said to bring good financial luck.

 Stone Street Historic District

Centered around Stone Street, several small blocks of 19th Century buildings and cobblestone streets is home to a thriving restaurant district. During warm months, tables spill out into the street and it's a popular destination for visitors and locals alike.

Did You Know?

A statue of King George III that once stood in Bowling Green was torn down by a mob in 1776, after the Declaration of Independence was read to Washington's troops. The statue was melted to make bullets for the revolution.

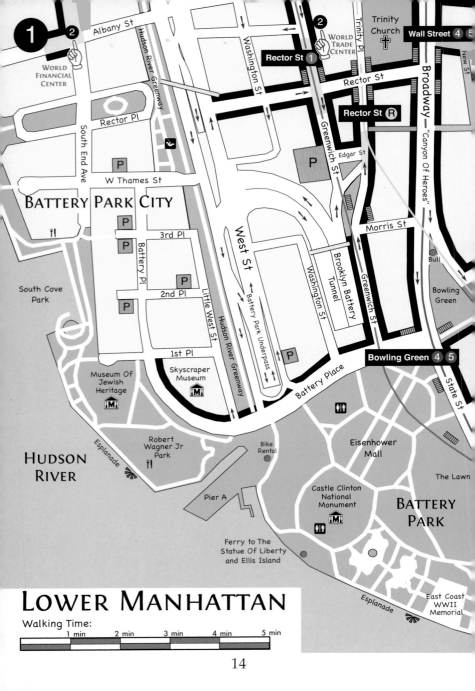

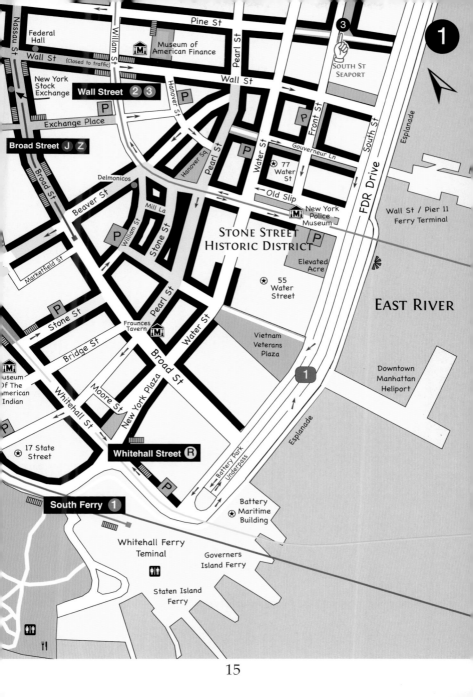

FINANCIAL DISTRICT & CIVIC CENTER MAP 2

This is the heart of finance and politics in New York City. The area features many of the city's most historic buildings as well as some of its most impressive architecture.

 City Hall

Still in use after two hundred years, New York's City Hall remains the center of the city's government. Free tours of this landmark building are available weekdays by reservation.

 Civic Center

To the east of City Hall is the vast Civic Center. Walk among the grand municipal and court buildings and take in the Roman Classical, Beaux Arts, and Federal Style architecture. In the lower level of the Municipal Building is the "City Store", which sells all things New York.

 Poet's House

The Poet's House is a free library containing over 50,000 volumes of poetry. It hosts many events throughout the year.

Brooklyn Bridge

With its Gothic-style arches towering above the East
River, the Brooklyn Bridge is a New York City icon.
Completed in 1883, the Brooklyn Bridge was the longest
suspension bridge in the world for many years. At 135
feet above the water, the wide pedestrian promenade
offers breathtaking views of the East River, lower Manhattan, and South Street Seaport. Take a walk across and
explore the quaint neighborhood of Brooklyn Heights.

Irish Hunger Memorial

If you walk north along the esplanade from the World
Financial Center, you will come upon the Irish Hunger
Memorial. This half acre plot is landscaped utilizing soil,
stones, and vegetation from the western coast of Ireland.
An authentic stone cottage from County Mayo has been
rebuilt on the site.

Irish Hunger Memorial

St. Paul's Chapel

Across Church Street from the World Trade Center site stands the historic Saint Paul's Chapel. Completed in 1766, it is New York's oldest public building in continuous use. George Washington worshipped here on his inauguration day, and his original pew has been preserved. While our founding fathers could not possibly imagine a future in which hundred-story skyscrapers would collapse into the church yard, they would be pleased to know St. Paul's Chapel miraculously escaped the attacks without even a broken window. It is said that an ancient sycamore tree, now known as the "miracle sycamore", deflected falling debris away from the church, but was itself destroyed. The tree's root has been preserved in a bronze sculpture and is displayed several blocks away in front of Trinity Church.

 African Burial Ground

The Civic Center is home to one of New York's most unexpected and interesting museums and memorials. In 1991, intact graves were discovered during the excavation for a new federal office building at Broadway and Duane Street. The remains of over 400 colonial-era African slaves were found at the site. This brought to public consciousness a forgotten burial ground that dates to the 1600s. A commemorative memorial and museum has been built at the site. It is estimated that between 15,000 and 20,000 bodies remain beneath the surrounding blocks and streets.

National September 11 Memorial & Museum

The top destination in the neighborhood, this memorial features two huge reflecting pools that outline the original footprints where the twin towers once stood. The site has become sacred ground for the millions of New Yorkers and visitors who come each year to pay their respects to those who lost their lives in the September 11, 2001 terrorist attacks. In addition to a museum and visitor center, the memorial features the largest man-made waterfalls in North America. Adjacent to the memorial, the new Freedom Tower at One World Trade Center rises to 1776 feet, making it the tallest building in New York City.

Fulton Center

Slated for completion in 2014, the Fulton Center will connect ten subway lines and provide transfers to the World Trade Center and PATH trains to New Jersey. There are multiple retail concourses planned, as well as connecting passages to the World Financial Center.

Did You Know?

When completed, the Brooklyn Bridge was hailed as the 8th wonder of the world, being one of the greatest engineering feats of the 19th century. Yet after its inauguration, much of the public still doubted its stability. In response, P.T. Barnum led a parade of 21 elephants, 7 camels, and 10 dromedaries across the bridge to prove its soundness.

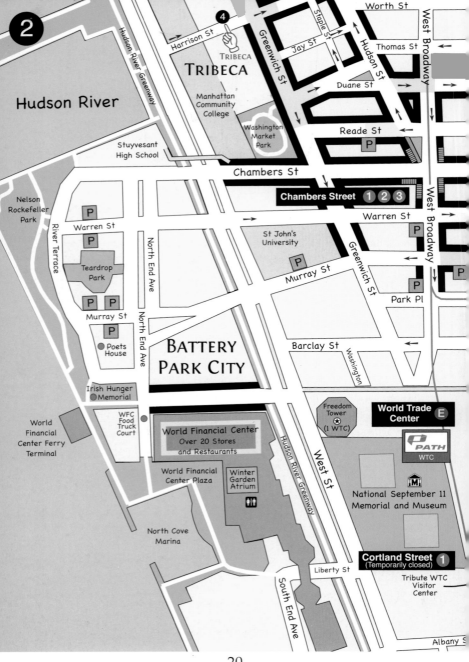

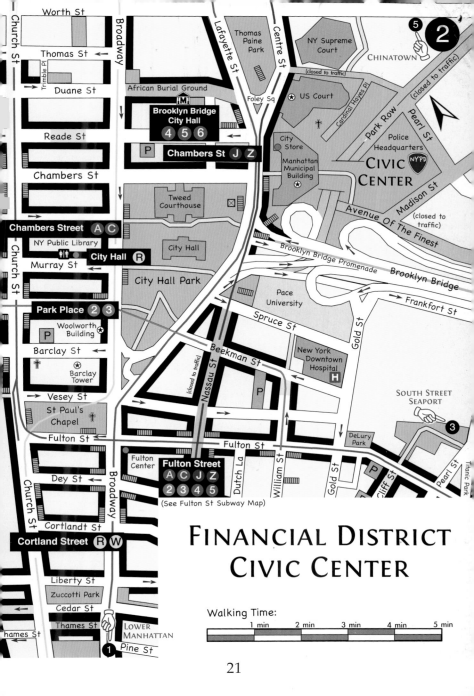

FINANCIAL DISTRICT CIVIC CENTER

Walking Time:

	1 min	2 min	3 min	4 min	5 min

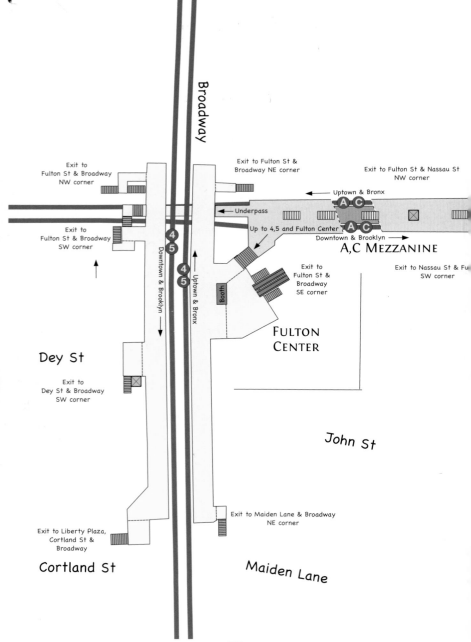

Broadway

Exit to
Fulton St & Broadway
NW corner

Exit to Fulton St &
Broadway NE corner

Exit to Fulton St & Nassau St
NW corner

Uptown & Bronx

Underpass

Exit to
Fulton St & Broadway
SW corner

Up to 4,5 and Fulton Center

Downtown & Brooklyn

A,C Mezzanine

Downtown & Brooklyn

Uptown & Bronx

Exit to
Fulton St &
Broadway
SE corner

Exit to Nassau St & Fu...
SW corner

Booth

Fulton
Center

Dey St

Exit to
Dey St & Broadway
SW corner

John St

Exit to Maiden Lane & Broadway
NE corner

Exit to Liberty Plaza,
Cortland St &
Broadway

Cortland St

Maiden Lane

FULTON STREET
SUBWAY STATION

Fulton Street
Ⓐ Ⓒ Ⓙ Ⓩ
② ③ ④ ⑤

Nassau St

Williams St

Exit to Fulton St &
Nassau St
NE corner

Fulton St

Ⓙ Ⓩ

Exit to
Fulton St
& Williams
St
SE corner

Exit to Fulton St &
Nassau St
SE corner

Downtown ← | → Uptown

Booth

Exit to Fulton
St & Williams
St SW corner

Because the street above is so narrow, the J,Z
Nassau Street Station is on two levels. The uptown
tracks and platforms are on the upper level, while
the downtown tracks & platforms are at the same
level as the A,C Mezzanine. Transfers are
accomplished below via the A,C platform.

Since the J,Z line effectively divides the
station, transfers between the 2,3 area and
the 4,5 area are also via the A,C platform.

2,3 MEZZANINE

②
③

Downtown & Brooklyn ↓

Exit to
Williams St

Exit to John St
and Nassau St
NE corner

John St

Exit to John St
and Nassau St
SE corner

Exit to
John St

Williams St

Uptown & Bronx

SOUTH STREET SEAPORT
MAP 3

Centered around the old Fulton Fish Market, Schermerhorn Row, and adjoining piers, the South Street Seaport is one of New York's biggest tourist destinations. Historic ships are on display in the harbor, right across from one of the city's busiest shopping and restaurant districts.

 Federal Reserve Bank

One of the twelve federal reserve banks, this location is famous for its gold vault, which is eighty feet below street level. Over half a million gold bars are stored there, worth over 250 billion dollars. It is the largest depository of monetary gold in the world. Free guided tours are available weekdays. Tickets must be purchased online.

 Schermerhorn Row and Seaport Museum

A row of nineteenth century counting houses which once served as offices for various shipping and import companies. Now part of the Fulton Street pedestrian mall, these buildings house the Seaport Museum as well as restaurants and shops. The Seaport Museum features three floors of galleries and exhibits related to New York's maritime history.

Seaport Area Dining

Explore the side streets around Peck Slip and discover some interesting gourmet restaurants as well as cozy maritime-themed taverns. See if you can find the Bridge Cafe - it claims to be one of New York's oldest drinking establishments.

  Pier 17

Currently undergoing renovations, the former Seaport Mall will re-open in 2015. The new space will feature a rooftop promenade, outdoor entertainment venues, retail shops, a food market, and waterfront restaurants.

 Bowne & Co. Stationers

A restored 19th century letter printer and gift shop operated by the Seaport Museum.

 Fulton Stall Market

A food, farmer, and craft market located at the former Fulton Fish Market building. Vendors line South Street where the old fish market stalls used to be. Open Sundays.

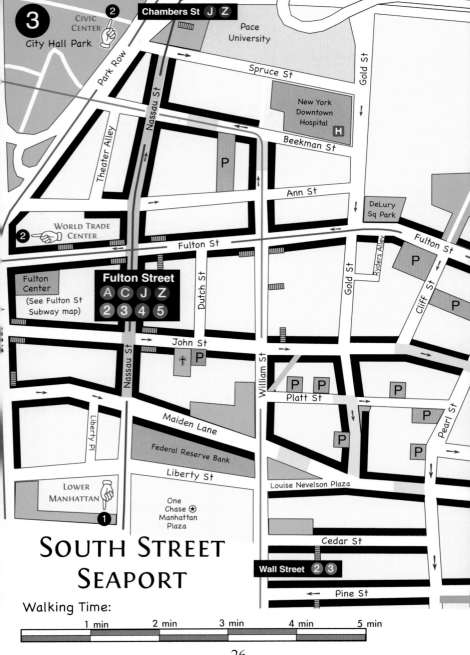

3 CIVIC CENTER

2

City Hall Park

Chambers St J Z

Pace University

Park Row

Spruce St

Nassau St

Gold St

New York Downtown Hospital H

Beekman St

Theater Alley

P

Ann St

DeLury Sq Park

2 WORLD TRADE CENTER

Fulton St

Fulton St

P

P

Cliff St

P

Fulton Center
(See Fulton St Subway map)

Fulton Street
A C J Z
2 3 4 5

Dutch St

Gold St

Ryders Alley

Nassau St

John St

P

William St

P P

P

Pearl St

Platt St

P

Liberty Pl

Maiden Lane

P

P

Federal Reserve Bank

Liberty St

Louise Nevelson Plaza

LOWER MANHATTAN

1

One Chase ✪ Manhattan Plaza

Cedar St

SOUTH STREET SEAPORT

Wall Street 2 3

Pine St

Walking Time:

| 1 min | 2 min | 3 min | 4 min | 5 min |

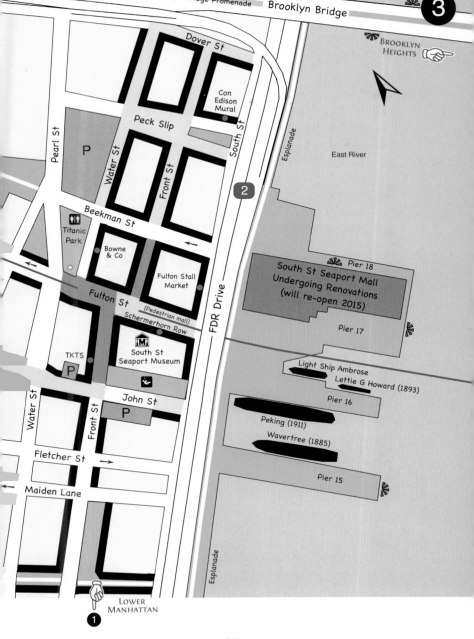

3

Brooklyn Bridge Promenade **Brooklyn Bridge**

BROOKLYN HEIGHTS ☞

Dover St

Con Edison Mural

Peck Slip

Pearl St

Water St

Front St

South St

Esplanade

East River

2

Beekman St

Titanic Park

Bowne & Co

Fulton Stall Market

Pier 18

South St Seaport Mall Undergoing Renovations (will re-open 2015)

Pier 17

FDR Drive

Fulton St

(Pedestrian mall)

Schermerhorn Row

TKTS

P

South St Seaport Museum

Light Ship Ambrose

Lettie G Howard (1893)

John St

P

Pier 16

Water St

Front St

Peking (1911)

Wavertree (1885)

Fletcher St

Pier 15

Maiden Lane

Esplanade

LOWER MANHATTAN

1

27

TRIBECA   MAP 4

Just to the north of the Financial District is the affluent residential neighborhood of Tribeca (**Tri**angle **Be**low **Ca**nal Street). Home to many celebrities and famous New Yorkers, Tribeca is one of Manhattan's most expensive neighborhoods. Greenwich Street serves as the area's main thoroughfare, with sunny outdoor dining and shopping a block from the waterfront.

Hudson River Park

 Harrison Street Row Houses

An historic block of restored 19th century Federal style row houses.

Bogartus Plaza

Just outside the Chambers Street subway stop, Bogartus Plaza is a good spot for relaxing or people-watching.

 Pier 25

Part of Hudson River Park, Pier 25 features a playground, skate park, volleyball, and inexpensive mini-golf. The view is not bad, either!

 Washington Market Park

This park features community gardens and large playgrounds. On Wednesdays and Saturdays there is a farmer's market on Greenwich Street, just outside the park.

 Shopping Tribeca

While Tribeca is not a mass market shopping destination per se, it is home to many unique stores. Explore the side streets between Greenwich and Hudson, where you'll find many little galleries and specialty shops.

Did You Know?

The Holland Tunnel was completed in 1927 and was one of the world's first ventilated tunnels. It is a National Historic Landmark and is used by over 35 million vehicles each year.

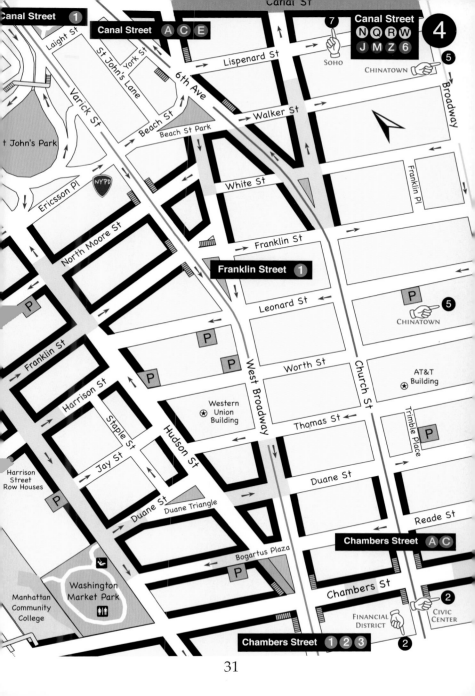

CHINATOWN MAPS 5 & 6

One of New York's most famous ethnic enclaves, Chinatown is rich with history and culture. On its narrow streets you'll find an array of specialty groceries, shops and restaurants.

Mott Street

Little Fuzhou

The eastern section of Chinatown is inhabited by a concentration of immigrants from the Fujianese Province
of China. The Bowery is the traditional dividing line
between Little Fuzhou and the Cantonese-dominated
"original" Chinatown to the west.

 Mahayana Buddhist Temple

This beautiful temple is open to the public and is a
peaceful respite from the often frantic pace of the neighborhood.

 Hua Mei Bird Garden

For a unique experience, visit this garden in the early
morning hours, when Chinese men display their Hua
Mei songbirds in beautiful bamboo cages.

Hua Mei Bird Garden

Museum of Chinese in America

Dedicated to the history and culture of the Chinese in America, the museum features many exhibits and programs.

 Eldridge Street Synagogue

Built in 1887, this meticulously restored landmark synagogue houses a museum celebrating its history.

 Chinese New Year Festival

Celebrated over the course of two weeks every February, the festival features parades, dancers, fireworks and food. Bring your earplugs - over 600,000 firecrackers are lit during the Firecracker Ceremony to scare away evil spirits!

 Columbus Park

A peaceful green space in the heart of Chinatown, where you will find Chinese residents engaged in card games, playing traditional Chinese instruments and practicing martial arts. It seems to be a world away from the hustle & bustle of the surrounding city.

 San Delano Roosevelt Park

Once a place to be avoided due to its reputation for crime and drugs, the park gained new life in the mid-1990s when hundreds of Chinese residents descended upon it with brooms, cleaning it up and chasing out the bad elements.

East River Park

One of several interconnected parks along the East River with sweeping views of the Manhattan and Williamsburg Bridges. The recently-renovated East River Amphitheater is home to the East River Music Project and hosts free concerts during the summer months.

 Canal Street

The western section of Canal Street is famous for its bargain-priced goods. The east end features jewelry stores. (Canal Street also has a reputation for counterfeit/grey market goods - if the deal seems too good to be true, it probably is.)

 Mott Street

By its very nature, Chinatown is one big marketplace. Mott Street is well known for its Oriental groceries and specialty shops.

Did You Know?

In the late 1800s the "Five Points" area was a dangerous slum. The narrow, winding Dyer Street was the site of gangland ambushes, earning the nickname "Bloody Angle". Times have changed, though - today Dyer Street is known as "Hair Street", home to many barber shops and beauty parlors.

LITTLE ITALY MAP 5

 Mulberry Street

The epicenter of Little Italy, this four-block stretch is home to over 35 Italian restaurants. This is a great place to come any time of year, but is especially nice in the warmer weather, when all the restaurants set up their tables on the sidewalk. Competition for customers is fierce, so expect every restaurant host you pass to try and sell you on their establishment. It's a lively area - between the locals and visitors from all over the world, this is one of the best people-watching spots in the city.

 Italian American Museum

Housed in a former immigrant bank, the museum is dedicated to the struggles and achievements of Italian Americans and their contributions to American culture.

 Feast of San Gennaro

Lasting 11 days every September, this is one of New York's most popular street festivals. Here you'll find a multitude of street vendors, games and entertainment. The central focus of the festival is a mass held at Most Precious Blood Church, followed by a religious procession where a statue of San Gennaro is carried through the street.

A replica of Michelangelo's "David" stands in front of a restaurant in Little Italy

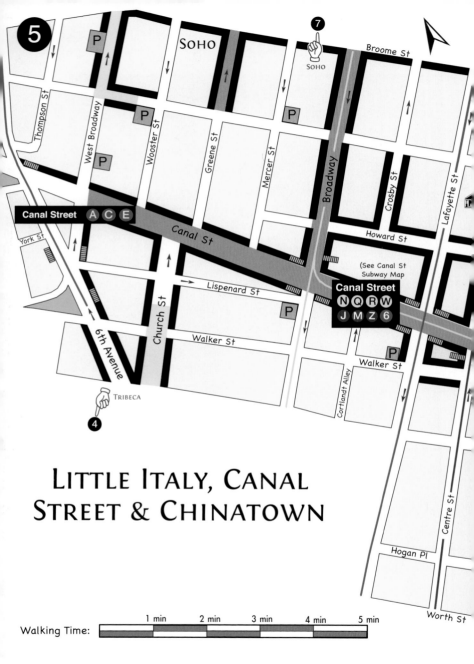

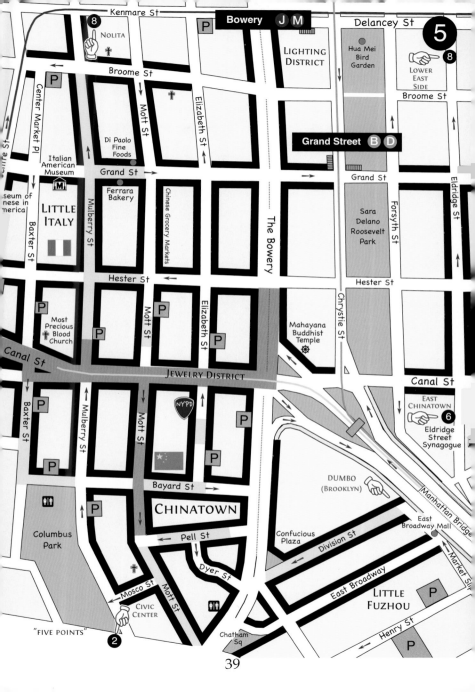

CANAL STREET
SUBWAY STATION

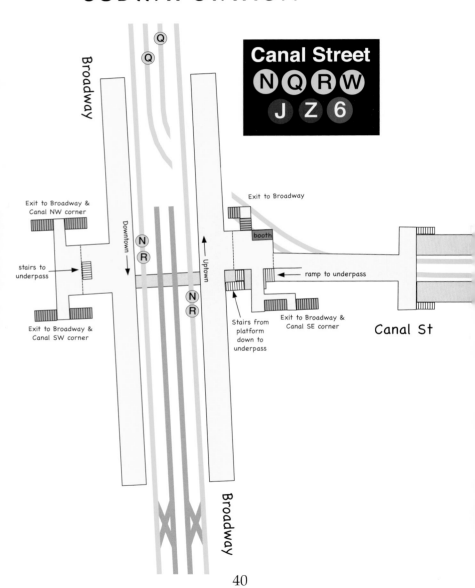

Broadway

Q

Q

Canal Street
N Q R W
J Z 6

Exit to Broadway &
Canal NW corner

Downtown

N
R

stairs to
underpass

Uptown

Exit to Broadway &
Canal SW corner

N
R

Exit to Broadway

booth

ramp to underpass

Stairs from
platform
down to
underpass

Exit to Broadway &
Canal SE corner

Canal St

Broadway

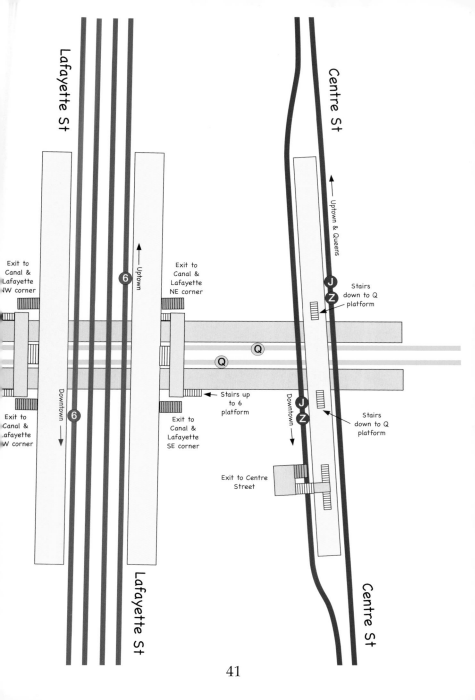

Lafayette St

Centre St

Exit to
Canal &
Lafayette
NW corner

Exit to
Canal &
Lafayette
NE corner

← Uptown

6

Uptown & Queens →

J
Z

Stairs
down to Q
platform

Q

Q

Downtown

Stairs up
to 6 ←
platform

6

J
Z

Exit to
Canal &
Lafayette
W corner

Exit to
Canal &
Lafayette
SW corner

Exit to
Canal &
Lafayette
SE corner

Downtown

Stairs
down to Q
platform

Exit to Centre
Street

Lafayette St

Centre St

41

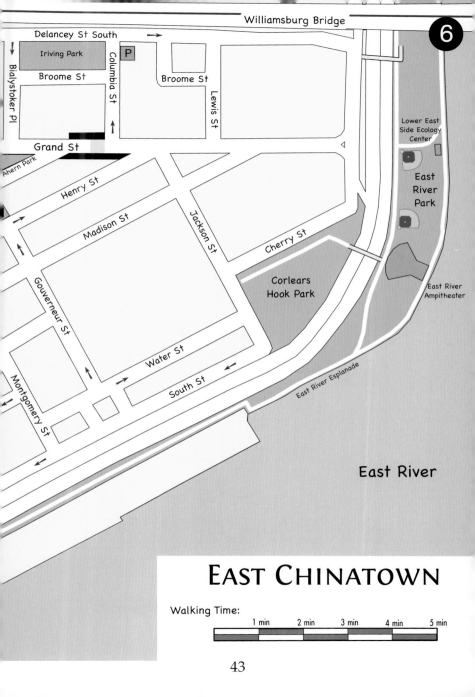

East Chinatown

SOHO   MAP 7

Soho (**So**uth of **Ho**uston) is New York's most popular downtown shopping district. Famous for its architecture, Soho's narrow cobblestone streets are home to the largest collection of cast iron buildings in the world. A popular construction material in the late 1800s, cast iron was cheap, strong, and easy to use for casting ornate architectural details. Some of the best examples are along Greene Street.

Haughwout Building

Haughwout Building

The Haughwout Building has had major historical significance for New York City - it was the first to feature a passenger elevator. The success of this new technology paved the way for the design and construction of skyscrapers.

 "Queen of Greene Street"

One of the most beautiful cast iron buildings in the neighborhood can be found at 20-30 Greene Street.

 "King of Greene Street"

Only slightly less ornate than its royal neighbor, this cast iron masterpiece sits at number 72 Greene Street.

 "Subway Map Floating on a New York Sidewalk"

This 87 foot long subway map is embedded in the sidewalk in front of the Soho Building at 110 Greene Street.

 Fire Museum

A beautiful beaux arts style 1904 firehouse, the museum features a large collection of historic firefighting equipment and memorabilia.

Hudson Square Food Truck Lot

While Soho offers many dining choices, an inexpensive al fresco lunch can be enjoyed during the summer months in this lot adjacent to Canal Street. An array of food trucks offer varied cuisine. Benches and tables are provided.

 Soho Shopping

Historic buildings house designer boutiques, galleries and brand-name retail stores. Shops are concentrated along Broadway and the blocks to the west.

 Getting Around

Connecting Soho to New Jersey is the Holland Tunnel. Completed in 1927, it was the first vehicular tunnel into Manhattan. Over 80 large fans provide ventilation and completely change the air in the tunnel every 90 seconds. Over 100,000 cars travel through the Holland Tunnel daily.

Did You Know?

In the 1950s, Soho's nickname was "Hell's Hundred Acres". A neglected industrial district, it continued to decline until artists began to take over the large loft spaces in the late 1960s. This new hip and artsy image soon attracted designers, restaurants and retailers which slowly transformed Soho into the fashionable neighborhood it is today.

"Queen of Greene Street"

NOLITA <small>MAP 8</small>

Once viewed as part of Little Italy, Nolita (**No**rth of **Lit**tle **Ita**ly) has recently come into its own as a chic shopping district. Boutiques line tree-shaded streets interspersed with galleries and restaurants.

 ## Old St. Patrick's Cathedral

Completed in 1815, this basilica was the original seat of the Roman Catholic Archdiocese of New York until 1879, when the new St. Patrick's Cathedral on 5th Avenue was completed. Movie fans will recognize the interior as the locale for several scenes from "The Godfather".

 ## Storefront for Art and Architecture

Founded in 1982, the Storefront features an ongoing program of exhibits, artist talks, and conferences relating to architecture and design. The unique building has become a contemporary architectural landmark.

 ## Dining

Besides the Italian restaurants that stretch up Mulberry Street from the south, many Nolita eateries can be found along Spring Street.

Lombardi's Pizza

Founded in 1905, Lombardi's claims to be the first pizzeria in the United States. It still uses its original coal-fired oven.

 Shopping

Explore the boutiques and specialty shops that line Prince, Mott, and Elizabeth Streets.

 Restaurant Supply District

Located on the eastern edge of Nolita, this interesting stretch of the Bowery is a great place to visit if you are looking for professional kitchen supplies.

Mulberry Street

LOWER EAST SIDE MAP 8

Many different immigrant groups called the Lower East Side home in the early part of the twentieth century. Overcrowding and slum conditions prevailed, but the melting pot of cultures left the neighborhood with a rich ethnic heritage. The area was once predominantly Jewish, and this influence is still apparent today. Many landmark Jewish businesses can still be found along Houston and Orchard Streets. Today, the Lower East Side is quickly losing its edgy feel as trendy shops, restaurants, and nightclubs are springing up on its once gritty streets.

 Lower East Side Visitor Center

Provides free information, maps and pamphlets to help visitors better discover the neighborhood.

 Essex Street Market

Established in the 1940s to get pushcarts off the streets, this gourmet food market features more than twenty independent vendors and three restaurants.

 Russ and Daughters

A family-owned business specializing in smoked fish, caviar, bagels, and sweets for over 97 years.

Economy Candy

This is a dream-come-true for candy lovers. Every imaginable kind of candy can be found here.

 Tenement Museum

A former tenement building at 97 Orchard Street houses the Lower East Side Tenement Museum. Restored to its early 20th century appearance, the museum seeks to educate visitors about immigrant life and the living conditions they endured. Neighborhood walking tours are also offered.

The Tenement Museum

Yonah Shimmel Knish Bakery

An authentic knishery, it has provided Jewish specialty foods to the neighborhood for over 100 years.

Yonah Shimmel Knish Bakery

 Katz Deli

The famous deli has been serving up their trademark sandwiches since 1888. Es Gesunt! (Yiddish: Eat in good health!)

 Freeman's Restaurant

While there are many interesting dining choices in the neighborhood, the most secret one is hidden at the far end of Freeman's Alley. Half the fun is getting there.

Lighting District

Need a unique lamp or a funky chandelier? Look no further than New York's lighting district on the Bowery, just south of Delancey Street.

 Orchard Street Shopping District

Still considered the main shopping thoroughfare of the neighborhood, Jewish-owned discount shops have given way to trendy boutiques. The street is closed to traffic on Sundays, when it is turned into a huge pedestrian shopping mall.

 Nightlife

The area around Rivington and Ludlow Streets is a popular nightlife district featuring all manner of bars, restaurants, and nightclubs.

Did You Know?

The Lower East Side of Manhattan was once the most densely populated place in the world.

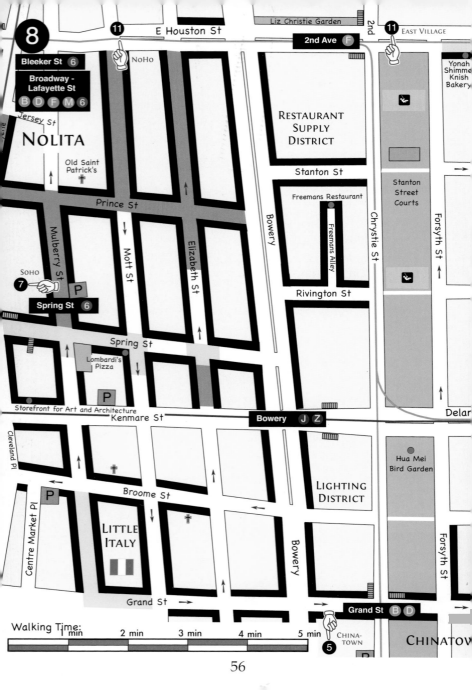

GREENWICH VILLAGE
MAPS 9 & 10

Greenwich Village is one of the most popular destinations in the city. With scores of restaurants, bars, beautiful historic streets, specialty stores, and nightclubs, "The Village" is worth visiting anytime of the day, week or year. Throughout the 20th century, Greenwich Village was known for its bohemian culture, and its "live and let live" attitude. The western portion of the neighborhood is known as the West Village, and was long the center of New York's gay and lesbian culture. Throughout the late 20th century, Christopher Street was known as the "Gay Main Street" of the USA. While some of this influence remains, this upscale neighborhood is in transition, with the gay community slowly migrating northward to Chelsea and Hell's Kitchen.

 Chess District

One of New York's most obscure mini-districts is the Chess District along Thomson Street. There are several shops that sell supplies and host games at all hours of the day and night.

 Cherry Lane Theater

Hidden away on a tiny winding street in the West Village is New York's longest continuously-running Off-Broadway theater. For those just looking for a place to take a quiet stroll, the surrounding neighborhood is one of the most beautiful and historic in the city.

Grove Street

Washington Mews

Just north of Washington Square Park is the tiny gated Washington Mews. Once a row of Victorian-era horse stables, the buildings were later converted to housing and offices for New York University.

 West Fourth Street Courts

While you are in the neighborhood, stop at the basketball courts at the corner of West 3rd St. and Sixth Ave. They feature some of the best street basketball in the world. Believe it or not, quite a few NBA stars got their start here. Find a spot along the fence and enjoy the game.

 Film Forum

A non-profit cinema that features foreign and independent films.

 Forbes Gallery

Houses the collection of Malcom Forbes, which includes antique toys, trophies, Faberge eggs, and historic documents.

 St. Luke's in the Fields

If you are in need of a peaceful green space, come enjoy the secret garden on the grounds of this Episcopal church. St. Luke's also hosts several choral and classical concerts throughout the year.

greenwich village

Washington Square Arch

Washington Square Park

Far outside the boundaries of the city back in the 1700s, the area that is now Washington Square Park was designated as a potter's field, where unknown people or slaves were buried. Thousands more were buried here as a hygienic measure during the yellow fever outbreaks in the early eighteenth century. As the city expanded northward, the graves remained, but the valuable real estate above them was turned into a military parade ground. It became a park in 1850 and was named for the country's first president, George Washington. The 77-foot marble arch was constructed in 1892, and immediately became a neighborhood landmark. The legendary "hangman's elm" in the northwest corner of the park is the oldest tree on the island of Manhattan, estimated at over 320 years old. Today, Washington Square Park is an excellent place to watch street performers, visit the dog park, or have an al fresco game at the chess tables. Take a walk along Washington Square North and appreciate the historic houses, and along University Place to see the Washington Square Windows, a year round non-profit public art gallery.

Hudson Street

Hudson Street is the main commercial thoroughfare of the far western part of the Village. You'll find a wide variety of restaurants and bars from West 11th St. south to Christopher Street. Aspiring writers should check out the White Horse Tavern, the bar of choice for Dylan Thomas, Norman Mailer, James Baldwin, and Jack Kerouac.

Sheridan Square

This is the heart of Greenwich Village. Restaurants, bars and nightclubs can be found in every direction, appealing to every taste. Just around the corner is the historic Stonewall Inn, which has catered to the gay and lesbian community since the 1960s. It was here that the 1969 Stonewall Riots began, sparking several nights of violence and protests in Greenwich Village. The event is considered to be the beginning of the gay rights movement in the United States.

 ### University Place

Just south of Union Square is a busy stretch of bars and restaurants. While this area is technically the Village, in reality it is part of the busy commercial shopping district around Union Square.

 ### Central Village

The area around Father Demo Square has two distinct vibes. To the east of Sixth Avenue and south of the park is a lively group of blocks that are home to all manner of bars and nightclubs. Due to the proximity of New York University, this area is hopping day and night. To the west of Sixth Avenue, along Carmine and Bedford Streets, you will find quiet gourmet restaurants tucked into the narrow tree-lined streets.

Bleeker Street

The main shopping thoroughfare of Greenwich Village is the famous Bleeker Street. No matter what your interest, there is something for everyone here. Fashion boutiques, specialty shops, bookstores, and gourmet shops share the street with bakeries, restaurants, and cafes.

Father Demo Square (corner of Bleeker & Carmine Streets)

 Antique District

A small antique district can be found on East 11th Street. The shops deal mainly in furniture and collectibles.

Shoe District

Another interesting shopping area is West 8th Street. Famous for its many shoe stores, this mini-district is concentrated mostly between 6th and 5th Avenues. If you keep walking east on 8th Street you'll eventually find yourself in the East Village, where 8th Street turns into Saint Marks Place.

 Nightlife

The section of Bleeker Street between MacDougal and Laguardia Streets is the center of New York's up and coming music scene. Musicians of all genres and talents perform nightly at some of the same nightclubs and coffeehouses that launched the careers of Bob Dylan, Jimi Hendrix, Barbara Streisand, Bette Midler, Joni Mitchell, Simon & Garfunkel, and Jackson Brown.

 Blue Note Jazz Club

Founded in 1981, the Blue Note is one of the most well-known jazz venues in the world, with performances nightly.

Did You Know?

It is believed that the remains of more than 20,000 people still lie beneath Washington Square Park.

greenwich village

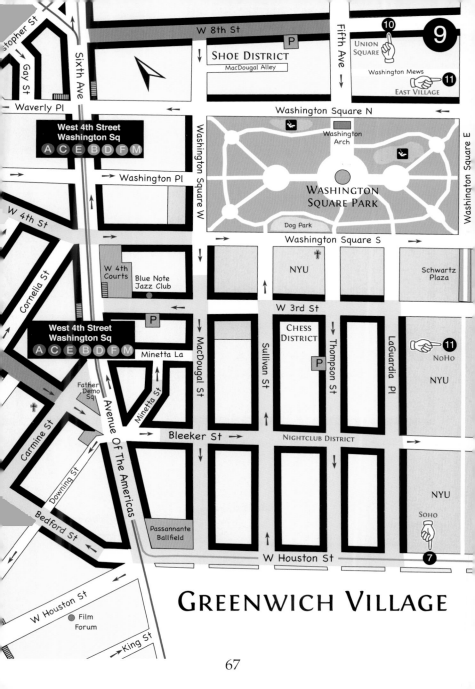

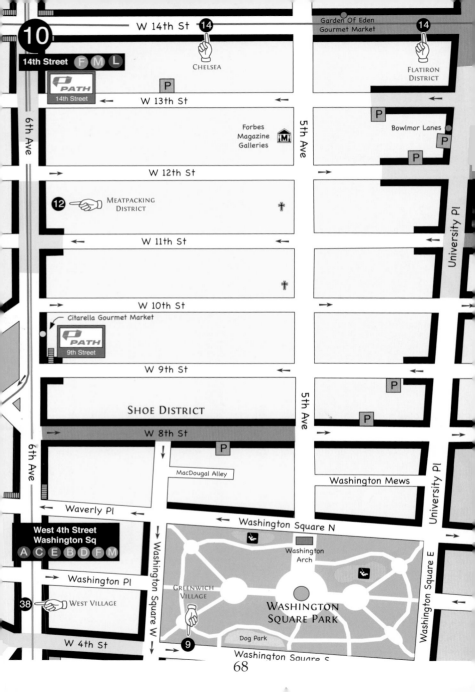

68

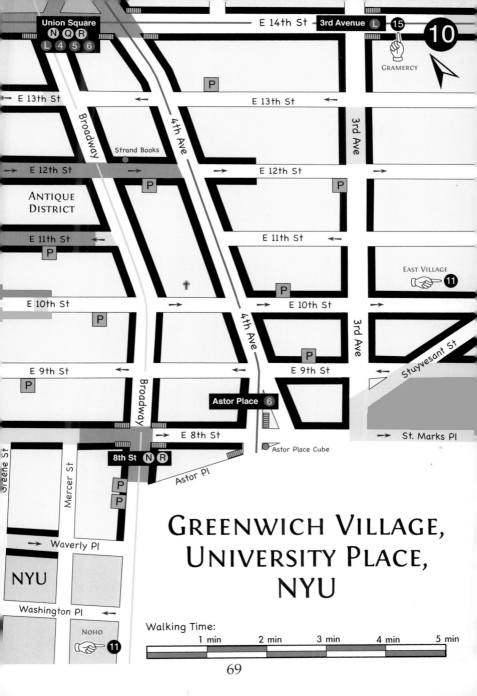

E 14th St · **3rd Avenue** Ⓛ · ⑮

Union Square
Ⓝ Ⓠ Ⓡ
Ⓛ ④ ⑤ ⑥

10

GRAMERCY

← E 13th St ←
E 13th St ←

Broadway

4th Ave

3rd Ave

Ⓟ

Strand Books

→ E 12th St →
E 12th St →

**ANTIQUE
DISTRICT**

Ⓟ

Ⓟ

← E 11th St ←
E 11th St ←

Ⓟ

Ⓟ

EAST VILLAGE
☞ ⓫

E 10th St →
→ E 10th St →

Ⓟ

Ⓟ

4th Ave

3rd Ave

Stuyvesant St

← E 9th St ←
← E 9th St
Ⓟ

Ⓟ

Astor Place ⑥

Greene St

Mercer St

Broadway

St. Marks Pl →

→ E 8th St
8th St Ⓝ Ⓡ
Astor Pl →
Ⓟ
Ⓟ

Astor Place Cube

→ Waverly Pl

NYU

Washington Pl ←

NoHo
☞ ⓫

GREENWICH VILLAGE,
UNIVERSITY PLACE,
NYU

Walking Time:
1 min   2 min   3 min   4 min   5 min

EAST VILLAGE MAP 11

The East Village is a neighborhood in transition, much like its neighbor to the south, the Lower East Side. Once overshadowed by drugs, poverty, and homelessness in the 1970s and '80s, the East Village has since rebounded into a hip and desirable residential neighborhood. While gentrification has transformed much of the area, it still keeps the best of its edgy and bohemian reputation.

St. Mark's Place

 Little Ukraine

The tiny enclave known as Little Ukraine is an area of Ukrainian-owned businesses near St. George's Church on 7th Street.

Tompkins Square Park

The centerpiece of the East Village, Tompkins Square Park first opened in 1834, and has had a long history of social unrest. In 1857, immigrants clashed with police over unemployment and food shortages, while in 1863 the park was the site of the deadly Draft Riots, protesting the Civil War draft. A hundred years later, there were antiwar demonstrations once again, this time protesting the Vietnam War. During the 1970s and '80s, the East Village went into a serious decline and Tompkins Square was home to more than 300 homeless people. This led to violence erupting again in 1989 when police tried to enforce a 1:00 am curfew, evicting the homeless population from the park. This sparked the infamous Tompkins Square Police Riot, in which residents and activists battled with the NYPD. This riot resulted in the park being closed for over a year and renovated. Today the park shows little evidence of its colorful past. Towering elms provide shade for lawns, playgrounds, and a popular dog run. The park hosts many concerts and events throughout the year.

 McSorley's Old Ale House

The oldest Irish pub in the city, McSorley's is a time capsule of old New York. It is a source of pride that the interior decor, including the memorabilia on the walls, has remained unchanged since 1910.

 **Curry Row**

A colorful collection of Indian restaurants along 6th Street, which wrap around onto 1st Avenue.

Curry Row

Saint Marks Place

The most well known street in the East Village, Saint Mark's Place is bohemia's main drag. There you will find specialty shops, tattoo and piercing parlors, bookstores, music stores, and antiques amongst the many cafes, bars, and nightclubs.

ALPHABET CITY   MAP 11

East of 1st Avenue, the north/south streets have letter names - Avenue A through Avenue D. This area is
known as "Alphabet City". Once predominantly Hispanic, the area still has a strong Latin flavor, especially
on the far eastern side. Ongoing gentrification is bring-
ing many young professionals to the area, and this is
reflected in the many bars and restaurants springing up
on Avenue C, as well as the area around Avenue B and
East 3rd Street. Alphabet City was the setting for the
Broadway musical "Rent".

 Museum of Reclaimed Urban Space

This unique museum is an archive of the local activism
that transformed the area. Tours of the neighborhood
are offered and are an excellent way of seeing the gardens and learning first hand this story of urban renewal.

 Community Gardens

Alphabet City has an interesting history and story of
transformation. Once a wasteland of garbage-filled
vacant lots and burned-out tenement buildings, the
residents worked with the city to get the buildings torn
down and create gardens in their place. Today, Alphabet City has more community gardens than any other
neighborhood in Manhattan. These beautiful green
spaces are a testament to the hard work and vision
of the people who took back their neighborhood and
paved the way for a complete revival of the area.

NoHo MAP 11

Noho (**No**rth of **Ho**uston) is situated between the East Village and Greenwich Village to the west. Originally a warehouse district, Noho is home to many loft-style buildings and historic architecture. Fashionable and hip today, the neighborhood features many galleries and is the center for much of the design, fashion and art industries. Mass market retail shops line Broadway near New York University.

 "The Alamo"

Otherwise known as the "Astor Place Cube" or just "The Cube", "The Alamo" is a neighborhood icon. Installed in 1967, the 1800-pound sculpture spins on its axis with a strong push.

 Astor Place Theater

Located in the historic Colonnade Row, the Astor Place Theater features works by aspiring and experimental playwrights.

 Joseph Papp Public Theater

Housed in the former Astor Library, this beautiful 1853 building contains five theater venues including "Joe's Pub", a cabaret-style restaurant.

Merchant House Museum

This Greek Revival row house was built in 1832 and is impeccably preserved inside and out. The museum provides a rare view into 19th century New York City life.

Merchant House Museum

 Strand Books

This epic bookstore has graced the corner of 12th Street and Broadway since 1927. It boasts over 18 miles of new and used books. It is the sole survivor of a historic "book row" that once stretched from Union Square to Astor Place.

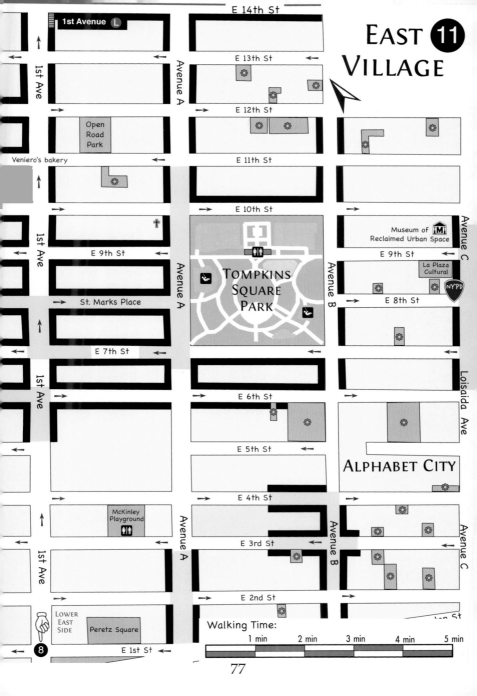

CHELSEA Maps 12, 13 & 14

Formerly a gritty waterfront industrial area of factories and tenements, Chelsea got a new lease on life as art galleries migrated here from Soho, and gay culture migrated here from the West Village. One of the most gay-friendly neighborhoods in Manhattan, this influence is most obvious along Eighth Avenue, where many gay-owned restaurants and shops can be found. The High Line elevated park cuts through the entire western side of the neighborhood, making this part of the city a popular destination.

 Chelsea Piers

On the Hudson River waterfront is the gigantic Chelsea Piers Sports and Entertainment Complex. These former passenger ship terminals have been transformed into New York's largest recreation center. The Chelsea Piers feature skating rinks, basketball, batting cages, a roller rink, driving ranges, swimming pools, bowling, spas, rock climbing, a marina and waterfront restaurants.

 West Chelsea Art District

Housed in reclaimed garages, warehouses and industrial space, the West Chelsea Art District is New York's most important art marketplace. Over 150 galleries can be found here, all open to the public.

Manhattan Kayak

Offers kayak and paddleboard lessons lessons and tours
of New York Harbor. Also provides boat storage and
access to the Hudson River

 Rubin Museum of Art

The largest collection of Himalayan art and artifacts in
the Western Hemisphere.

 Center for Jewish History

This archive preserves millions of documents spanning
over 700 years of Jewish history. In addition, the collection includes artwork, textiles, ritual objects, recordings,
films and photographs.

 Fashion Institute of Technology

On the northern border of Chelsea where it joins the
Garment District, you'll find the Fashion Institute of
Technology. This internationally renowned college of
art, design and fashion is closely allied with New York's
fashion industry. The complex houses a museum that
is open to the public, and features rotating exhibits of
clothing, shoes, accessories, textiles, documents and
photographs relating to fashion.

Hudson River Park

The Chelsea waterfront is one of the most popular areas of Hudson River Park. The wide esplanade features beautiful gardens and provides sweeping views of the Hudson River. Pier 62 features a skate park and carousel, while Pier 64 is dedicated to open green space, and even boasts a grove of oak trees. A little farther north is Pier 66, home to a cafe and several historic vessels.

 Chelsea Antiques District

On the northern edge of the neighborhood is the Chelsea Antiques District, which is concentrated along 25th Street. The best time to visit is during the weekend, when the 25th Street Antiques Market and Antiques Garage are open. Unique items from all over the world and every time period can be found here.

 Fur District

Just south of Penn Station and Madison Square Garden is the quickly-disappearing Fur District. Shops can be found on West 29th and 30th Streets, mostly around Seventh Avenue. If you look carefully, you'll find architectural details on several buildings depicting foxes, minks, and squirrels, harkening back to a time when there were over 800 fur manufacturers and dealers squeezed into these blocks.

Sixth Avenue

Mass market retail shopping is centered around 6th Avenue and is home to the Limelight Marketplace. This Gothic church-turned-shopping-center was formerly the famous Limelight nightclub. The building now holds over 60 small high-end retail shops.

Limelight Marketplace

Did You Know?

Pier 59 in Chelsea was the never-reached destination of the RMS Titanic when it sank in 1912. The Carpathia dropped off the Titanic's life boats there before docking at Pier 54 to unload passengers and survivors.

MEATPACKING DISTRICT
MAP 12

To the southwest of Chelsea is the Meatpacking District.
Originally an industrial area of slaughterhouses and
meat packers, this now uber-hip destination has gone
through several colorful incarnations. In the early part of
the 20th century, this was the center of food distribution
in New York and was known as the Gansevoort Market.
When changes in food distribution rendered much of
the neighborhood obsolete, it declined along with the
rest of the city in the 1970s and '80s. The neighborhood
became known for its decaying industrial landscape,
sex-oriented nightclubs, and gay prostitution. As the
city recovered, the new millennium saw the spectacular
rise of the Meatpacking District as a fashionable neighborhood. Trendy nightclubs moved in, and upscale
retail followed. Cobblestone streets are now lined with
classy boutiques, and restaurants and clubs abound,
making this formerly run-down corner of Manhattan
one of New York's premiere nightlife spots.

 Chelsea Market

Housed in a converted factory building, this huge
indoor market features over 30 gourmet food stores and
several restaurants.

The High Line

Playing a huge role in the area's revival is the High Line Park. Originally built as an elevated freight line to serve Manhattan's industrial west side, the High Line fell into disuse and was eventually taken out of service by the early 1980s. A rusting behemoth throughout the next decade, nature began to claim the decaying structure. This fact was not lost to preservationists that lobbied to turn the so-called eyesore into a public park. Over the next several years, many people came together to create one of New York's most popular open spaces. Featuring an artistic design of natural and industrial elements, the park forms a greenway above the streets of the Meat-packing District and Chelsea. It opened to the public in 2009.

The High Line

MEATPACKING DISTRICT

Walking Time:

| 1 min | 2 min | 3 min | 4 min | 5 min |

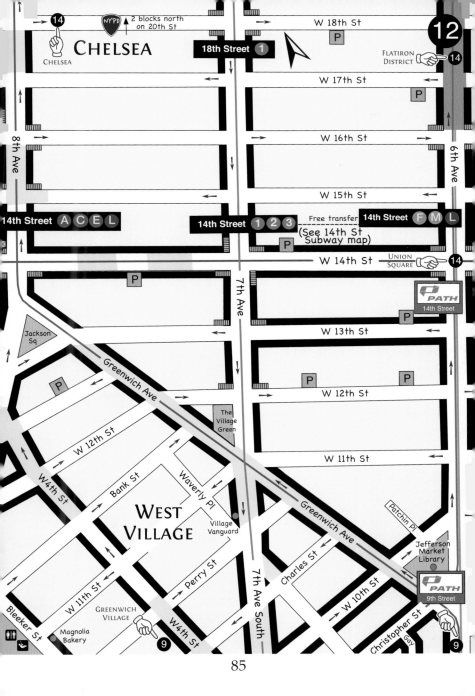

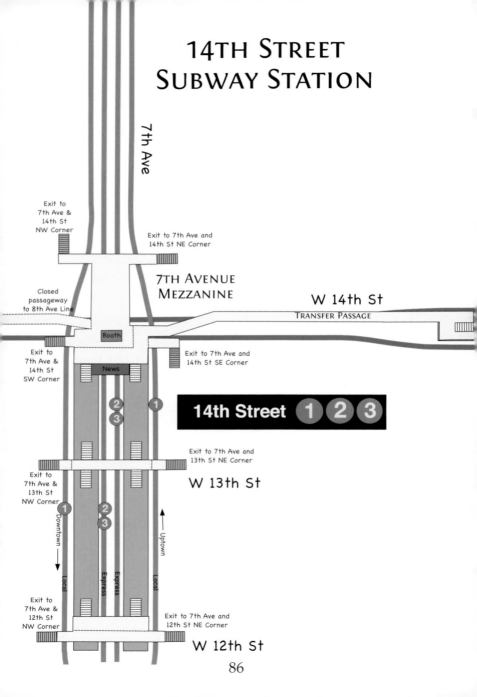

14TH STREET
SUBWAY STATION

7th Ave

Exit to
7th Ave &
14th St
NW Corner

Exit to 7th Ave and
14th St NE Corner

7TH AVENUE
MEZZANINE

Closed
passageway
to 8th Ave Line

W 14th St

TRANSFER PASSAGE

Booth

Exit to
7th Ave &
14th St
SW Corner

News

Exit to 7th Ave and
14th St SE Corner

14th Street ① ② ③

Exit to 7th Ave and
13th St NE Corner

Exit to
7th Ave &
13th St
NW Corner

W 13th St

Downtown →

Uptown →

Local

Express

Express

Local

Exit to
7th Ave &
12th St
NW Corner

Exit to 7th Ave and
12th St NE Corner

W 12th St

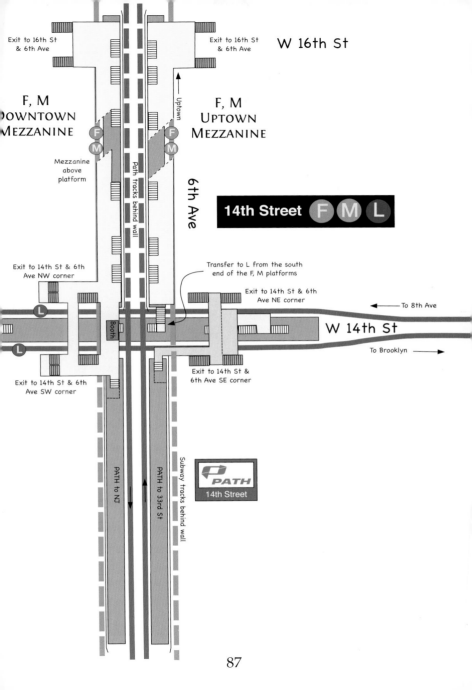

Exit to 16th St & 6th Ave

Exit to 16th St & 6th Ave

W 16th St

F, M DOWNTOWN MEZZANINE

F, M UPTOWN MEZZANINE

Uptown

Mezzanine above platform

Path tracks behind wall

6th Ave

14th Street F M L

Exit to 14th St & 6th Ave NW corner

Transfer to L from the south end of the F, M platforms

Exit to 14th St & 6th Ave NE corner

To 8th Ave

Booth

W 14th St

To Brooklyn

Exit to 14th St & 6th Ave SW corner

Exit to 14th St & 6th Ave SE corner

PATH to NJ

PATH to 33rd St

Subway tracks behind wall

PATH

14th Street

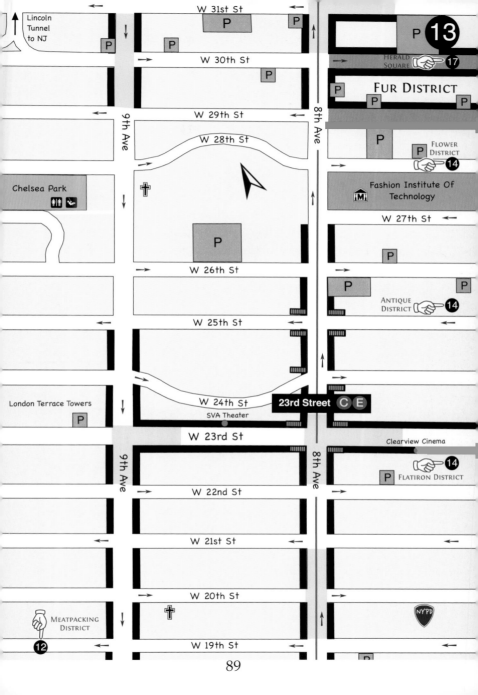

FLATIRON DISTRICT MAP 14

An upscale shopping district, the area is named for its most famous skyscraper - the Flatiron Building. Originally called the Fuller Building, the unique three sided structure resembled a flatiron and was so named by the public. Built in 1903, it was for some time the tallest building in the world. Legend has it that the air currents around the building would lift the Victorian era skirts, so crowds of young men used to gather on 23rd Street in hopes of witnessing the wind exposing a lady's ankle. The chances were not bad, considering the number of ladies that frequented this shopping district a hundred or so years ago.

 ## Eataly

On the northwest corner of 23rd Street and Broadway is the enormous Italian food market known as Eataly. Inside you will find an array of vendors selling all manner of gourmet specialties. The building is home to several Italian-themed restaurants and a rooftop bar as well.

 ## Madison Square Park

Across from the Flatiron Building is Madison Square Park. This historic square was the site of the first public baseball games in the 1840s. Today it offers a quiet respite from the frantic hustle of the city, with its beautiful fountains and 19th century statues.

Ladies Mile

A century ago, this section of Fifth Avenue was known as "Ladies Mile" and featured many famous department stores. Although many of the names have changed since then, the opulent buildings that line 5th Avenue still house many upscale and luxury retailers.

Flatiron Building

Union Square   Map 14

Where Broadway meets 14th Street is the famous pedestrian plaza of Union Square. When it was opened in 1836, it marked the northern border of the city. Today the park is the site of New York's biggest farmer's market (Mon, Wed, Fri, Sat) as well as various street fairs throughout the year. It's surrounded by mass market retail stores, and many restaurants can be found on the side streets.

 Theodore Roosevelt Birthplace

This townhouse on East 20th Street has been converted to a museum dedicated to the life of Theodore Roosevelt, the only U.S. president born in New York City. Exhibits include memorabilia and restored period rooms.

Union Square Park

GRAMERCY PARK
MAPS 14 & 15

To the east of Union Square is Gramercy Park, referring both to the exclusive private park and the neighborhood that surrounds it. An upscale and elegant area of the city, the neighborhood is full of beautiful architecture - so beautiful in fact, that East 19th Street between Irving and 3rd Avenue is known as "Block Beautiful".

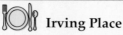 **Irving Place**

A small restaurant district, Irving Place features many fine eateries including the famous "Pete's Tavern", which is one of several New York drinking establishments that claim to be the oldest in the city.

Block Beautiful

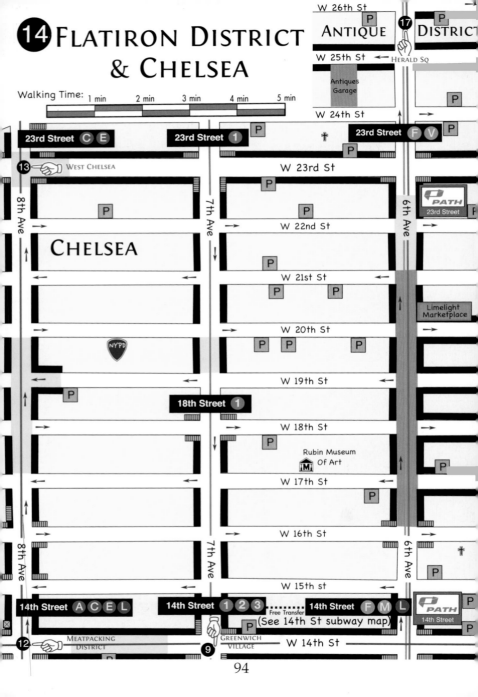

ANTIQUE ⑰ DISTRICT

Walking Time: 1 min 2 min 3 min 4 min 5 min

W 26th St

W 25th St ← HERALD SQ

Antiques Garage

W 24th St

23rd Street C E | 23rd Street 1 | 23rd Street F V

⓭ WEST CHELSEA | W 23rd St

P PATH 23rd Street

CHELSEA

W 22nd St

W 21st St

Limelight Marketplace

W 20th St

NYPD

W 19th St

18th Street 1

W 18th St

Rubin Museum Of Art

W 17th St

W 16th St

W 15th st

14th Street A C E L | 14th Street 1 2 3 ····· 14th Street F M L

Free Transfer (See 14th St subway map)

P PATH 14th Street

⓬ MEATPACKING DISTRICT | ⑨ GREENWICH VILLAGE | W 14th St

8th Ave

7th Ave

6th Ave

94

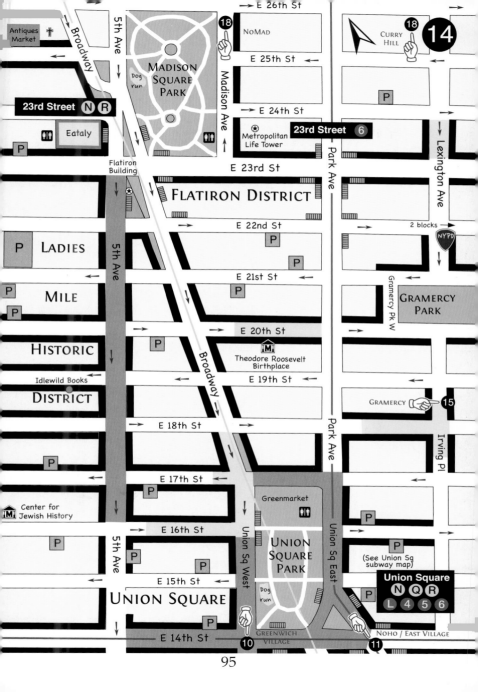

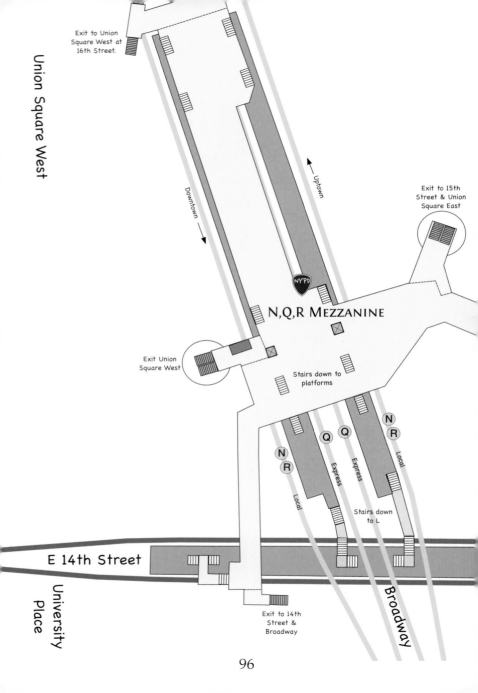

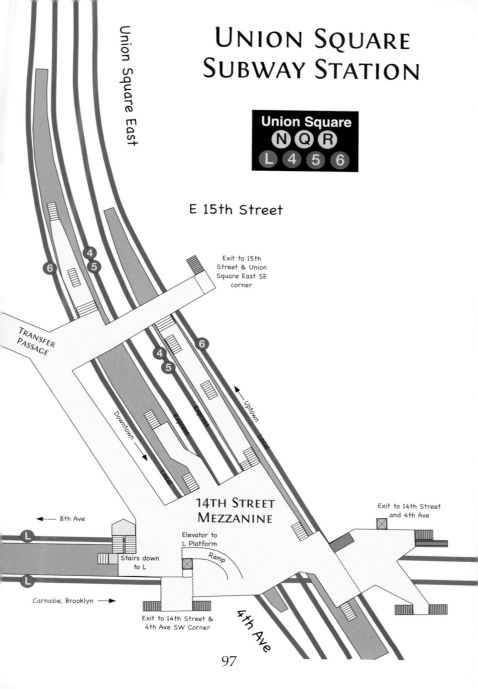

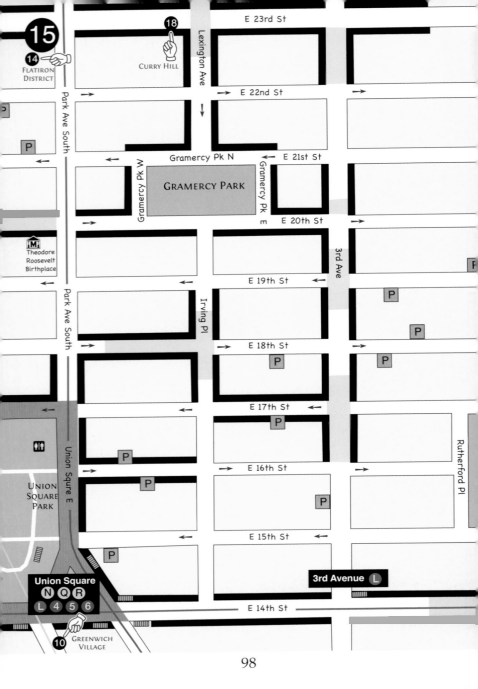

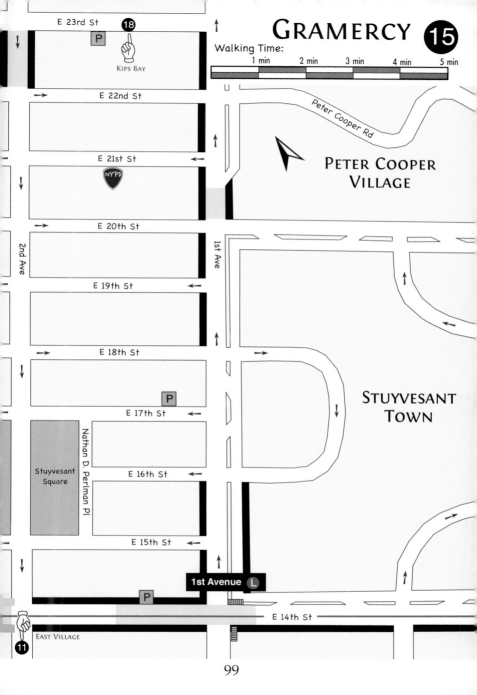

E 23rd St

P

18

KIPS BAY

Walking Time:

| 1 min | 2 min | 3 min | 4 min | 5 min |

E 22nd St

Peter Cooper Rd

PETER COOPER VILLAGE

E 21st St

NYPD

E 20th St

2nd Ave

1st Ave

E 19th St

E 18th St

STUYVESANT TOWN

P

E 17th St

Nathan D. Perlman Pl

E 16th St

Stuyvesant Square

E 15th St

P

1st Avenue L

E 14th St

11

EAST VILLAGE

Hell's Kitchen, Clinton & Midtown West Maps 16, 20 & 23

The name "Hell's Kitchen" was coined by local police in the 1880s to describe the run down tenements that once existed around 39th Street and 10th Avenue. These streets were so dangerous and crime-ridden that an officer once commented: "This place is Hell." His partner replied: "No, this is worse...this is Hell's kitchen." The name stuck.

While the neighborhood's sinister reputation is all in the past, it went through more hard times along with the rest of the Times Square area in the 1970s and '80s. As part of revitalization efforts, real estate developers created the name "Clinton", which they thought sounded more welcoming and upscale. While the traditional northern boundary of Hell's Kitchen was West 42nd Street, today either name is acceptable when referring to the entire area between 34th Street and 59th Street.

 Jacob Javits Center

The Javits Center is Manhattan's largest convention center, with over 675,000 square feet of exhibition space. It hosts many conventions, trade shows, and special events throughout the year.

Circle Line Tours

One of New York's most popular sightseeing cruises, Circle Line offers several tour options, including their well known trip around the entire island of Manhattan.

 57th Street Greenmarket

Serves the west side of Manhattan with fresh seasonal food from local farms. Open Wednesdays and Saturdays from 8 am to 5 pm.

 Downtown Boathouse

Provides free public access to New York Harbor for kayakers. Also hosts free classes and kayaking trips.

 U.S.S. Intrepid Sea, Air & Space Museum

Housed in a World War II era aircraft carrier, the museum features many exhibits, including dozens of military aircraft, the Concorde, the U.S.S. Growler submarine, and the space shuttle Enterprise.

 Pier 84

Another popular area of the Hudson waterfront, Pier 84 is the largest pier in Hudson River Park and features many amenities including public lawns, play areas, a boat launch, bike rentals, and a dog run. The pier hosts many concerts and events throughout the year.

Dewitt Clinton Park

A small park with ballfields, chess tables, a playground, and rest rooms.

 Dining in Hell's Kitchen

Fortunately for visitors and residents alike, the "Hell" is all in the past, but the "Kitchen" remains. This area of New York is now well known for its large restaurant district. It includes "Restaurant Row" on West 46th Street, as well as a long stretch of 9th Avenue where you'll find over a dozen blocks packed with bars and restaurants of every kind. Within walking distance from Times Square and the Theater District, this is a great place to come eat before a show or have a cocktail afterwards.

Restaurant Row

Auto Dealer District

Where can you visit all the popular automobile dealer showrooms on foot? Look no further than 11th Avenue near DeWitt Clinton Park. All the world's major manufacturers are squeezed into a few short blocks.

 Gateway to New York

Hell's Kitchen is one of the main entry points for the city, with an abundance of transportation options. The Port Authority Bus Terminal serves both commuter and long distance buses, while the Lincoln Tunnel brings automobile traffic in from New Jersey. Trains terminate at Penn Station, and the waterfront is home to ferry and passenger ship terminals. If you are arriving from the west, it is likely that Hell's Kitchen will be the first part of New York you see.

Port Authority Bus Terminal

HELL'S KITCHEN

Walking Time:

| | 1 min | 2 min | 3 min | 4 min | 5 min |

W 40th St

LINCOLN TUNNEL TO NEW JERSEY **495**

Outbound Tunnel

11th Ave

W 39th St

Center Tunnel

Inbound Tunnel

W 39th
Street Ferry
Terminal

W 38th St

P

P

W 37th St

Jacob K. Javits
Convention Center

W 36th St

Pier 76
Tow Pound

W 35th St

W 34th St

Hudson River Greenway

W 33rd St

Hudson
River

11th Ave

West Side Rail Yards

Hudson River Greenway

High Line

High Line (Proposed)

W 30th St

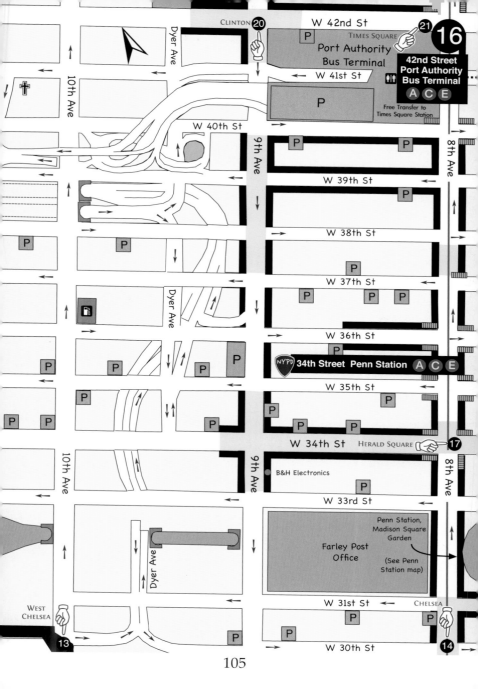

105

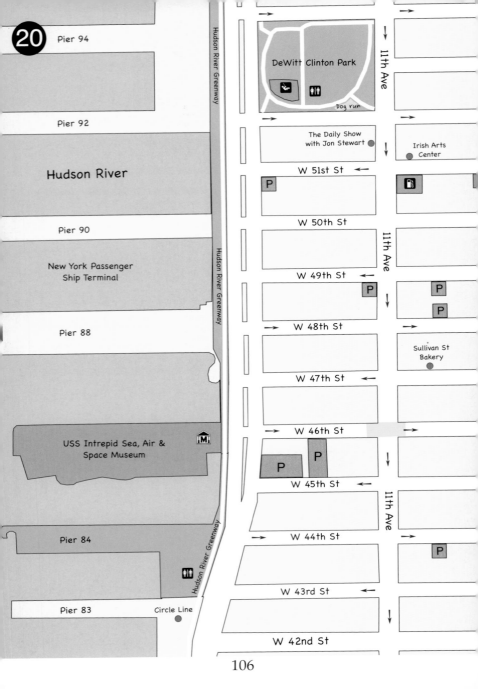

20 Pier 94

Pier 92

Hudson River

Pier 90

New York Passenger
Ship Terminal

Pier 88

Hudson River Greenway

DeWitt Clinton Park

Dog Run

11th Ave

The Daily Show
with Jon Stewart

Irish Arts
Center

W 51st St

P

P

W 50th St

11th Ave

W 49th St

P

P

P

W 48th St

Sullivan St
Bakery

W 47th St

W 46th St

USS Intrepid Sea, Air &
Space Museum

iMi

P

P

W 45th St

11th Ave

Pier 84

W 44th St

P

W 43rd St

Hudson River Greenway

Pier 83

Circle Line

W 42nd St

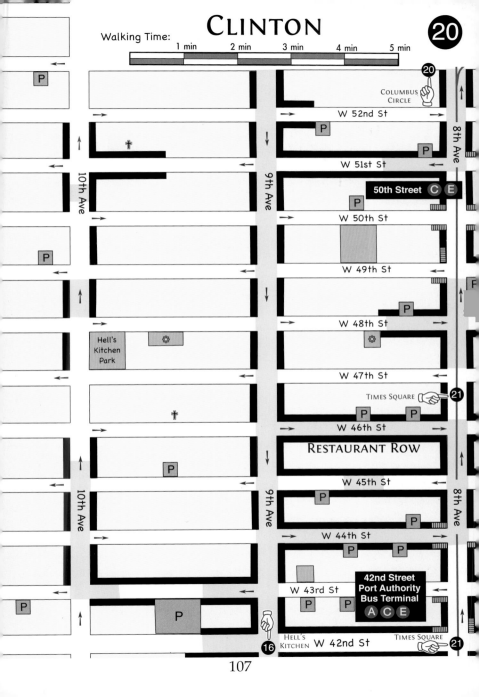

CLINTON

Walking Time:

1 min 2 min 3 min 4 min 5 min

20

COLUMBUS CIRCLE

W 52nd St

W 51st St

50th Street C E

W 50th St

W 49th St

W 48th St

Hell's Kitchen Park

W 47th St

TIMES SQUARE 21

W 46th St

RESTAURANT ROW

W 45th St

W 44th St

42nd Street Port Authority Bus Terminal

A C E

W 43rd St

HELL'S KITCHEN W 42nd St TIMES SQUARE 21

16

10th Ave

9th Ave

8th Ave

F

Walking Time:

1 min   2 min   3 min   4 min   5 min

Thelonius Monk Cir.

W 62nd St

P

W 61st St

West End Ave

West Side Highway

P

W 60th St

P

P

Hudson River

W 59th St

Joe DiMaggio Highway

12th Ave

Pier 99

W 58th St

Pier 98

W 57th St

P

Pier 97

P

Downtown Boathouse

W 56th St

Car Dealer District

11th Ave

P

W 55th St

W 54th St

Pier 94

DeWitt Clinton Park

Dog run

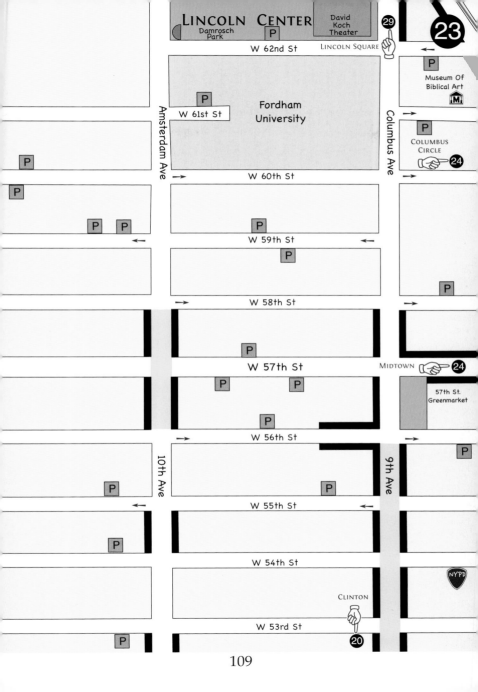

LINCOLN CENTER
Damrosch Park
David Koch Theater
P
LINCOLN SQUARE
29
23

W 62nd St

Museum Of Biblical Art
P
iMi

Fordham University
P
W 61st St

Amsterdam Ave

Columbus Ave

COLUMBUS CIRCLE
P
24

W 60th St

P

P
W 59th St

P
W 58th St

P

P

P

P
W 57th St
MIDTOWN
24

P

P

P
57th St. Greenmarket

P
W 56th St

10th Ave

9th Ave

P
P

P
W 55th St

P

P
W 54th St

NYPD

CLINTON

P
W 53rd St
20

Herald Square Map 17

The center of mass market shopping for over 100 years, Herald Square is more vibrant than ever. Shopping streets stretch in every direction, catering to every imaginable style and budget.

 Flower District

Along 28th Street is the famous Flower District. An oasis of florists, plant vendors, and garden centers, the sidewalks are often lined with greenery, creating a lush jungle between 6th and 7th Avenues.

 Koreatown

East of Broadway on 32nd Street is the area known as Koreatown. Korean stores, restaurants, and nightclubs are packed tightly into this block, often stacked atop each other on the upper stories of buildings. All things Korean can be found here, and surprisingly, the restaurants and bars are open 24 hours a day, 7 days a week.

 Empire State Building

New York's most famous landmark, the Empire State Building was built in 1931, and is the second tallest skyscraper in New York at 1454 feet. (The Freedom Tower is tallest at 1776 feet). At night, the top thirty stories are illuminated in colors that reflect the day or season. Visit the observatories on the 86th and 102nd floor for a spectacular bird's eye view of the Big Apple.

Madison Square Garden

New York's premier sports, entertainment, and concert venue. It is the home of the N.Y. Knicks basketball team and the N.Y. Rangers hockey team.

 Macy's Thanksgiving Day Parade

The world's most famous parade is broadcast from the Grandstand at Herald Square, which is also the parade's end point.

 Macy's

Immortalized in the film "Miracle On 34th Street", the Macy's flagship store is the crown jewel of the Herald Square shopping district. The massive building, built in 1902, covers an entire city block and is host to ten stories of fashions and home goods. Take note of the wooden escalators, still in operation after more than a century.

 Manhattan Mall

Built on the former site of Macy's archrival Gimbel Brothers, the Manhattan Mall features over 60 stores and 15 eateries. There is an entrance right from the Herald Square subway station; during inclement weather you never even have to step outside.

 34th Street

Name brand stores dominate 34th Street on the blocks to the east and west of Herald Square.

Garment District

West of 7th Avenue, explore the cross streets above 34th Street and discover a wide array of women's fashion shops that make up the Garment District. A little farther north, around 39th and 40th Streets, you'll find a concentration of shops that specialize in fabric and sewing supplies. The giant needle & button sculpture on the corner of 40th and 7th Avenue is a neighborhood icon.

 Penn Station

Below Madison Square Garden is the confusing maze known as Penn Station. Fortunately you now have a detail map to help you find your way around (see pp. 118-119). Much of the confusion stems from the fact that within the confines of the station you have four different companies operating trains on twenty-nine different tracks. Amtrak runs long distance routes, New Jersey Transit runs local routes to NJ, the Long Island Railroad runs to (surprise) Long Island, and the MTA has two subway stops (A,C,E trains and 1,2,3 trains) all squeezed together in one massive complex with absolutely abysmal signage. Once you get your bearings, you'll find that within the station are many retail shops, fast food restaurants, and a few bars.

Did You Know?

While you are waiting for your train in Penn Station, you may be lucky enough to see one of the many musicians that perform as part of the MUNY, or "Music Under New York" program. These talented folks must pass an audition and then be selected out of hundreds of hopefuls for this exclusive opportunity. MUNY performers can be seen at many of the major subway stations as well. All the musicians and bands play for free and make these confusing underground places a little nicer, so please remember to tip them!

Needle & Button Sculpture in the Garment District

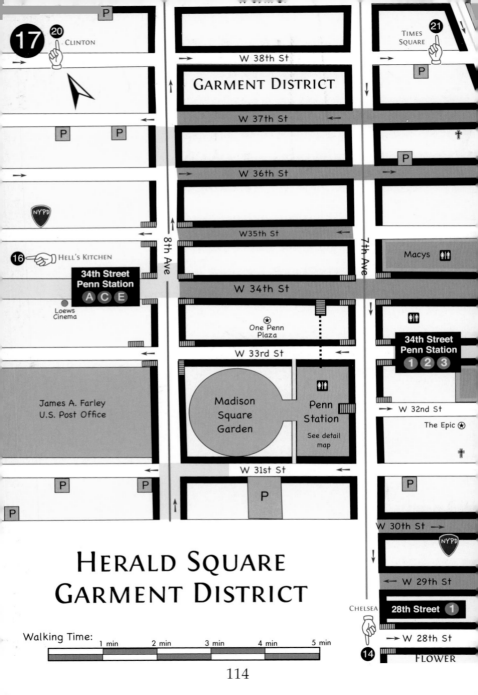

P

17 **20** CLINTON

TIMES SQUARE **21**

P

W 38th St

GARMENT DISTRICT

W 37th St

P **P**

P

W 36th St

NYPD

W 35th St

16 HELL'S KITCHEN

Macys

34th Street Penn Station
A **C** **E**

W 34th St

Loews Cinema

★ One Penn Plaza

34th Street Penn Station
1 **2** **3**

W 33rd St

James A. Farley U.S. Post Office

Madison Square Garden

Penn Station

See detail map

W 32nd St

The Epic ★

W 31st St

P

P **P**

P

P

W 30th St

NYPD

P

W 29th St

HERALD SQUARE
GARMENT DISTRICT

CHELSEA

28th Street **1**

W 28th St

14 FLOWER

Walking Time:

| 1 min | 2 min | 3 min | 4 min | 5 min |

114

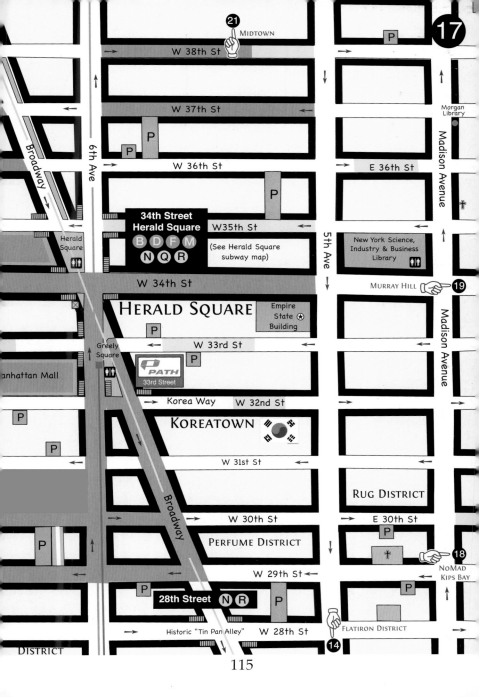

New York City Skyline
Photo credit: Christopher Bailey

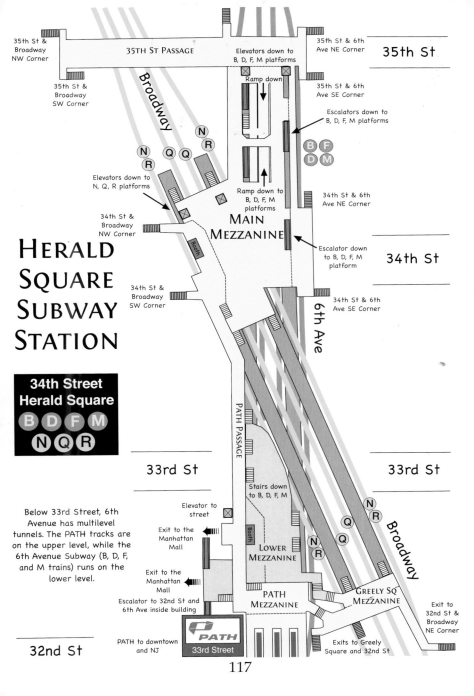

PENN STATION

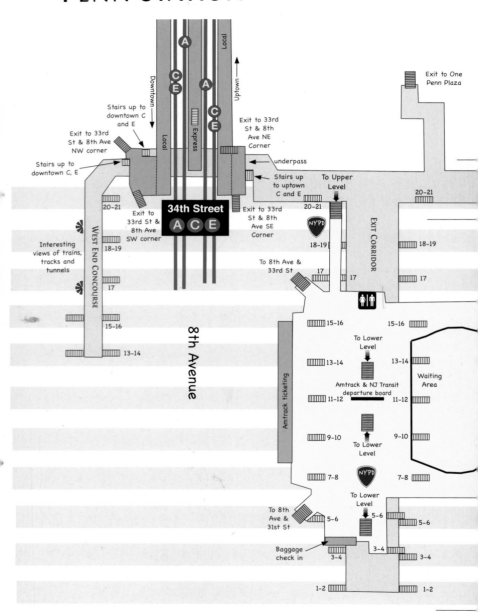

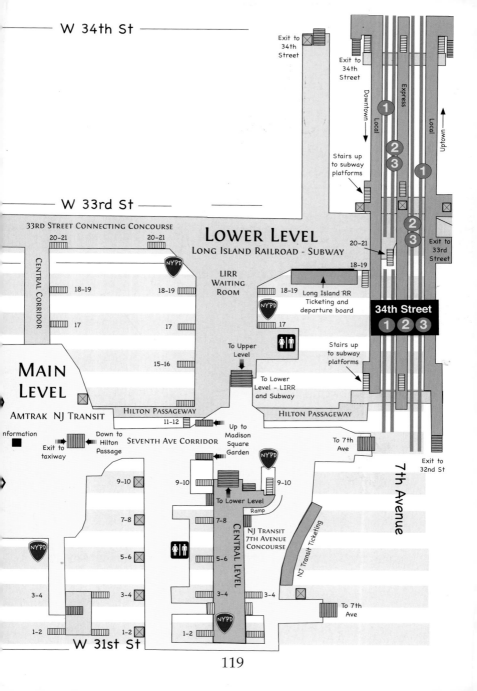

W 34th St

Exit to 34th Street

Exit to 34th Street

Downtown

Local

Express

Local

Uptown

1

2
3

1

Stairs up to subway platforms

W 33rd St

33RD STREET CONNECTING CONCOURSE

20-21   20-21

LOWER LEVEL
LONG ISLAND RAILROAD - SUBWAY

20-21

18-19   18-19   NYPD

18-19

LIRR WAITING ROOM

18-19   Long Island RR Ticketing and departure board

17   17   NYPD   17

2
3

Exit to 33rd Street

CENTRAL CORRIDOR

15-16

To Upper Level

34th Street
1 **2** **3**

To Lower Level - LIRR and Subway

Stairs up to subway platforms

MAIN LEVEL

AMTRAK NJ TRANSIT

HILTON PASSAGEWAY

HILTON PASSAGEWAY

nformation

Exit to taxiway

Down to Hilton Passage

SEVENTH AVE CORRIDOR

11-12

Up to Madison Square Garden

To 7th Ave

Exit to 32nd St

9-10   9-10   NYPD   9-10

7th Avenue

To Lower Level

Ramp

NJ TRANSIT 7th AVENUE CONCOURSE

7-8   7-8

CENTRAL LEVEL

NJ Transit Ticketing

5-6   5-6

3-4   3-4   3-4   3-4

To 7th Ave

1-2   1-2   1-2

NYPD

NYPD

W 31st St

NoMad MAP 18

To the north of Madison Square Park is the aptly named neighborhood of NoMad (**No**rth of **Mad**ison Square). Primarily an office and residential area, there are several interesting mini-districts nestled in here.

 Repertorio Espanol

A Spanish theater dedicated to the arts and heritage of the Hispanic community.

 Museum of Sex

One of New York's most interesting museum experiences, the Museum Of Sex is dedicated to the history, evolution, and cultural significance of human sexuality. Exhibits are presented in an educational format, but expect some explicit content nevertheless. Visit the downstairs bar and cafe for aphrodisiac-themed food and drinks.

 Curry Hill

The area gets its name from the many Indian restaurants that are concentrated along Lexington Avenue and 27th and 28th streets.

Rug District

If you explore the blocks surrounding 30th and 31st Streets in the vicinity of Madison Avenue, you will find shops selling all kinds of rugs, carpets, and floor coverings.

KIPS BAY MAP 18

To the east of NoMad is the neighborhood known as Kips Bay. Named after Dutch settler Jacobus Kip, much of the land east of First Avenue was once a natural bay with several streams running into it. This was the site of the British landing when they invaded New York in 1776 during the early months of the Revolutionary War. The namesake bay has long since been filled in, and Jacobus Kip's farm is now the site of an upscale residential neighborhood.

 Kips Bay Dining

A lively stretch of authentic New York bars and restaurants can be found along Third Avenue.

 Visual Arts Museum

This small exhibit space can be found in the lobby of the School of Visiual Arts.

Murray Hill MAP 19

North of 34th street is the neighborhood known as Murray Hill. Primarily a residential area, the neighborhood was named after the Murray family farm that once graced a (since flattened) hilltop here. Mrs. Murray would later play a part in American history, delaying the British army by inviting the officers for tea as they marched northward from Kips Bay. This allowed George Washington and the Continental Army to safely retreat to the fortified heights in present day Harlem.

 Museum of Tolerance

A multimedia museum that challenges visitors to confront racism and prejudice in the world. There is special focus upon the understanding of the Holocaust.

 Morgan Library Museum

Houses a collection of rare books, manuscripts, drawings and other works of art. The museum also features a performance hall, reading room, cafe, restaurant, and gift shop.

 Murray Hill Dining

As in Kips Bay to the south, Third Avenue is the main destination street for dining and nightlife. Due to its proximity to the midtown tunnel, Murray Hill's night spots are popular with young people from Queens and Long Island.

Did You Know?

Hidden behind a gate on East 36th Street in Murray Hill, Sniffen Court was originally built as an alley of carriage houses and stables. They were converted to residences in the 1920s. Rock & roll historians will recognize the street as the photo location of the Doors' "Strange Days" album cover.

Sniffen Court

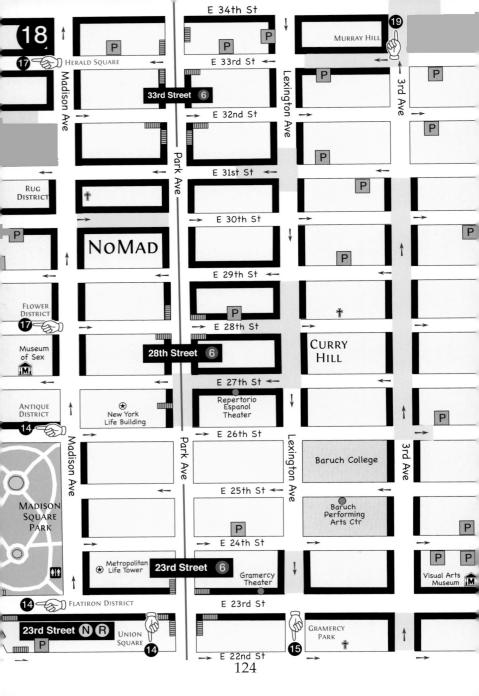

E 34th St

P · P · P

MURRAY HILL

19 ☝

🖐 **17** · HERALD SQUARE

E 33rd St

Madison Ave

33rd Street ⑥

P · 3rd Ave

P

E 32nd St

P

E 31st St

RUG DISTRICT · ✝

E 30th St

P

NoMad · P

E 29th St

FLOWER DISTRICT

🖐 **17** · ✝

E 28th St

Park Ave

28th Street ⑥

CURRY HILL

Museum of Sex

E 27th St

ANTIQUE DISTRICT

Repertorio Espanol Theater

🖐 **14** · New York Life Building

P

E 26th St

Lexington Ave

Baruch College

E 25th St

MADISON SQUARE PARK

Baruch Performing Arts Ctr

P

E 24th St

P · P

Metropolitan Life Tower

23rd Street ⑥

P

Gramercy Theater

Visual Arts Museum

🖐 **14** · FLATIRON DISTRICT

E 23rd St

23rd Street Ⓝ Ⓡ · UNION SQUARE

🖐

🖐 GRAMERCY PARK ✝

P · **14** ☝

15 ☝

E 22nd St

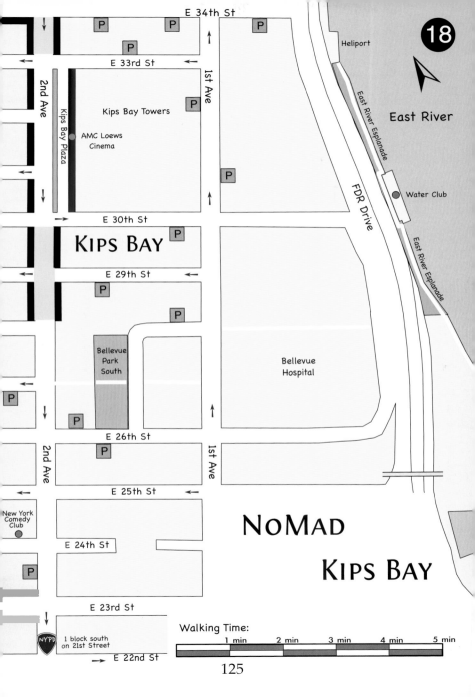

E 34th St

P P P

E 33rd St

2nd Ave

Kips Bay Plaza

Kips Bay Towers

P

AMC Loews
Cinema

1st Ave

Heliport

East River Esplanade

East River

18

Water Club

FDR Drive

East River Esplanade

E 30th St

KIPS BAY

P

E 29th St

P

P

Bellevue
Park
South

Bellevue
Hospital

P

P

E 26th St

2nd Ave

P

1st Ave

E 25th St

New York
Comedy
Club

NoMad

E 24th St

P

KIPS BAY

E 23rd St

NYPD

1 block south
on 21st Street

E 22nd St

Walking Time:

1 min   2 min   3 min   4 min   5 min

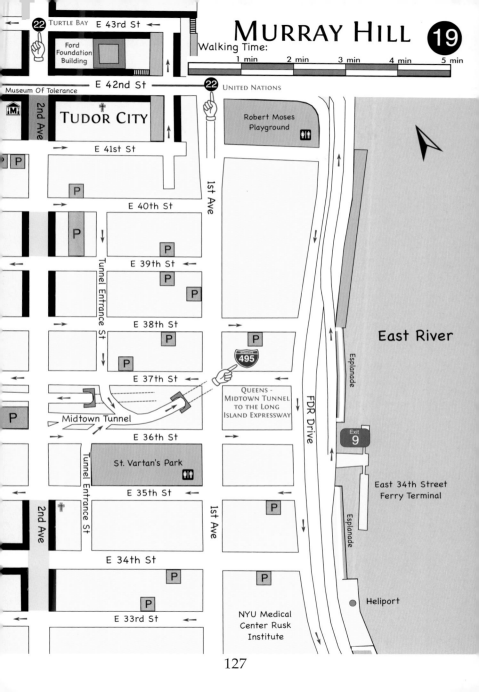

TIMES SQUARE & THEATER DISTRICT MAP 21

Known as the "Crossroads Of The World", Times Square will take your breath away with its awe inspiring display of advertisements, multicolored lights, giant screens, and animated signs. With over forty million visitors each year, Times Square remains the most popular tourist destination in North America. The scale of everything - the buildings, the lights, and the crowds - is so over the top, pictures can't capture it. Times Square has to be seen to be believed, so make sure you walk through here at least once. If you need a place to rest after all that walking, Broadway between 42nd and 47th Streets has been turned into a giant pedestrian mall, complete with tables and chairs for those that need to sit and take it all in.

Times Square

Times Square Visitor Center

Provides visitors with information on the area's many attractions. Theater tickets and tours are also available. A mini museum displays the former New Year's Eve Ball, as well as artifacts from the area's X-rated past. Former peep show booths now play videos about the neighborhood's history.

 Discovery Times Square

Presents traveling exhibitions on various historical events and cultural phenomena. Former exhibits have included the Titanic, King Tut, Dead Sea Scrolls, and Harry Potter.

 Ripley's Believe It Or Not "Odditorium"

A circus sideshow of human oddities as well as a museum of the weird, including genuine shrunken heads.

 Diamond District

Ready to pop the question? Then head over to the Diamond District on 47th Street. You'll know you are there by the huge diamond-shaped lights on either end of the block. The street is lined with jewelry shops and exchanges where over 2,500 independent dealers ply their trade. According to one source, ninety percent of all diamonds that enter the United States go through this tiny district.

Theater District

The famous Broadway theater district can be found on the side streets west of Times Square. With over fifty theaters packed into a few small blocks, this is the entertainment capital of the world. Like the song says, "If you can make it here, you'll make it anywhere"! Expect to see the best of the best. Buy tickets online, at the theater box office, or try your luck at the TKTS kiosk at 47th Street in the middle of Times Square. TKTS sells discounted tickets the day of the show. Be aware that many of the popular Broadway shows are sold out months in advance, so plan accordingly.

Theater District

 Madame Tussaud's

A wax museum featuring amazing life-like recreations of celebrities, historical figures, and politicians.

42nd Street

With its red light district past just a memory, 42nd Street has morphed into a wholesome and exciting destination. Hotels, theaters, and restaurants line the famous section between 8th Ave and Broadway.

42nd Street

 New York Public Library

At the intersection of 5th Ave and 42nd Street is the main building of the New York Public Library. The second largest library system in the U.S., (the Library Of Congress is the biggest), the grand marble building was constructed between 1908 and 1911. The interior is majestic, with high frescoed ceilings, chandeliers, and massive windows. The library provides access to over 65 million items. Across 5th Avenue from the library, stretching along 41st Street, is the "Library Walk". For two blocks, you can find bronze plaques embedded in the sidewalk, featuring quotes and illustrations from famous works of literature.

New Year's Eve in Times Square

Times Square lives up to its reputation as the crossroads of the world on New Year's Eve. Over a billion people around the world watch as the biggest party on the planet gets underway every December 31st. Over a million revelers fill the streets around Times Square, with crowds on Broadway and Seventh Avenue stretching as far as Central Park. There are performances and celebrity appearances which start around 6:00 pm and continue through the night until 11:59 pm, when the New Year's Eve Ball drops and heralds in the new year. If you are planning on coming to Times Square on New Year's Eve, it is important to plan ahead. Get there early (revelers start arriving around 3:00 pm) and dress warmly. Go to www.timessquarenyc.org for detailed information.

Did You Know?

The Times Square New Year's Eve Ball is twelve feet in diameter and weighs over 5 tons. It is covered by 2,688 Waterford crystals and lit by over 32,000 LEDs. When the clock strikes twelve on New Year's Eve, a blizzard of confetti is released from rooftops throughout Times Square. Many of these colored pieces of paper have wishes written on them. You can add your own New Year's wish by visiting the "wishing wall" at the Times Square Visitor's Center.

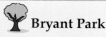 Bryant Park

Adjacent to the New York Public Library is Bryant Park, which has the distinction of being the most densely occupied park in the world. It's built entirely over the New York Library's underground archives, features restaurants, free wifi, and winter ice skating, and hosts many events and concerts throughout the year.

Times Square Dining

There is a multitude of dining choices for all tastes and budgets in the Times Square area. As one might expect, many cater to the theater and tourist crowd. If you feel a little rushed, it's mainly because restaurants in this area are accustomed to getting theater-goers in and out before showtime. A word of caution - check your bill and make sure the gratuity is not added automatically. Some restaurants attempt to protect their servers from notoriously bad-tipping tourists. Don't be one of those offenders - twenty percent is the standard gratuity in New York City. If the service was outstanding, tip a little more.

Did You Know?

Times Square was once the center of New York's sex industry. Many can remember when the streets of this area were lined with X-rated video shops, porn theaters and peep shows. A massive revitalization in the 1990s transformed it into the family-friendly destination it is today.

Times Square Shopping

Dominated by souvenir shops and larger than life store-fronts, shopping in Times Square is primarily geared towards tourists. There is plenty for the kids, too. Besides all the cartoon characters and superheroes wandering the crowds posing for pictures, the Disney Store is here, as well as a dedicated Hershey Store and M&M World. For a real eye opener, visit the Toys R Us "Center Of The Toy Universe" flagship store and experience a dazzling array of toys and displays, from an indoor Ferris wheel to a life size dinosaur.

 Beneath Times Square

Down below all the noise and lights of Times Square is the city's busiest and biggest subway station. The massive complex connects eleven different subway lines on several different levels. A maze of passages and stairways can confuse all but the most subway-savvy New Yorker. Recently renovated, the Times Square station is clean, well lit, and has clear signage. If you are not in a hurry, take the time to appreciate live entertainment by street performers as well as the mosaic artwork throughout the station. There are even clean rest rooms on the main mezzanine (you'll have to ask an attendant for the key). It's a big and complicated place, so while you are walking through the station, take a moment to think about this author getting lost in here back in the '80s, when it was a dimly lit, filthy, and scary domain of drug dealers, prostitutes, pickpockets, and the homeless. Think about how much he wished he had a map like the one you have on pp. 144-145!

Times Square

ROCKEFELLER CENTER
MAP 21

Just to the east of Times Square is the massive Rockefeller Center. A city within the city, the complex features some of New York's most famous landmarks, historic buildings, and top attractions.

Rockefeller Center Fountain Statue of Prometheus

 Radio City Music Hall

Home of the legendary Rockettes, Radio City Music Hall features shows and concerts year round.

 NBC Studios

Take the NBC Studio tour and see where some of television's most famous programs such as The Today Show and Saturday Night Live are created. If you time your visit right, you may witness a free concert in the plaza.

Top of the Rock

Want to get a bird's eye view of the Big Apple? Then head up to the "Top Of The Rock" observation deck. At 70 stories above the plaza below, the views from the three level, year-round rooftop deck are unrivaled.

Rockefeller Center

Christmas at Rockefeller Center

One of the most important events in New York City during the holiday season is the lighting of the of the Rockefeller Center Christmas Tree. Usually scheduled in early December, the celebration draws tens of thousands to the plaza and surrounding streets. The event includes performances by top artists and is watched by hundreds of millions around the world. The tree remains lit until January 6th.

Rockefeller Center Christmas Tree

 Rockefeller Center Dining

While there is an abundance of eateries in the area, Rockefeller Center has many restaurant choices on site, as well. Head to the lower concourse and you'll find several restaurants overlooking the skating rink (which turns into outdoor seating in the warmer months).

138

Rockefeller Center Shopping

Rockefeller Center features over 50 retail stores in the sprawling complex encompassing the blocks between 48th and 51st Streets, as well as in the lower level concourse beneath. You will find many major brand name stores as well as restaurants and gift shops.

Beneath the Rock

A great rainy day destination, the huge Rockefeller Center complex has its own entrance directly from the Sixth Avenue subway (B,D,F,M lines). A vast maze of underground passageways connects the Concourse Level to the subway and many of the surrounding buildings. Take a look at the detail map on pp. 148-149 and you'll navigate the place like a pro.

Getting Around Rockefeller Center

If you are driving in Manhattan during the holidays, (which is already a bad idea to begin with), you especially want to avoid the Rockefeller Center/5th Avenue area. The traffic will quickly dampen your holiday cheer, and you'll be honking and cursing along with the rest of the motorists stuck in holiday gridlock!

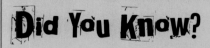

The Rockefeller Center Tree is lit with over 30,000 lights. The star atop the tree is almost ten feet in diameter and weighs 550 pounds.

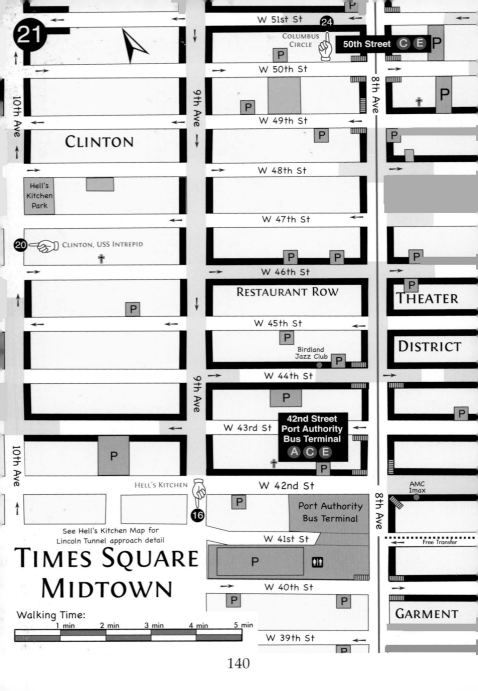

TIMES SQUARE
MIDTOWN

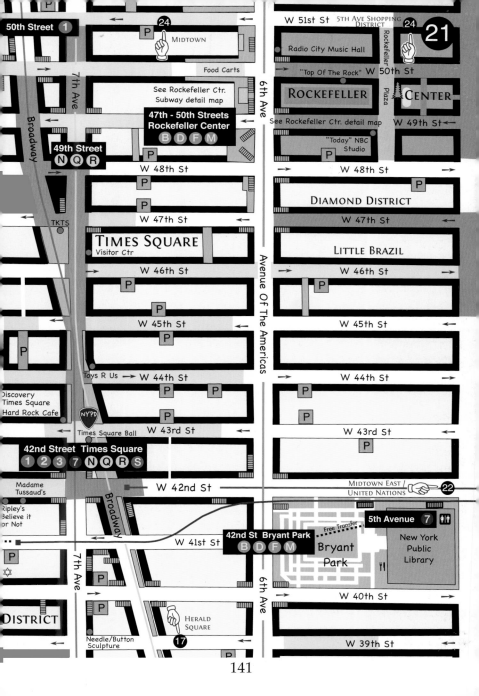

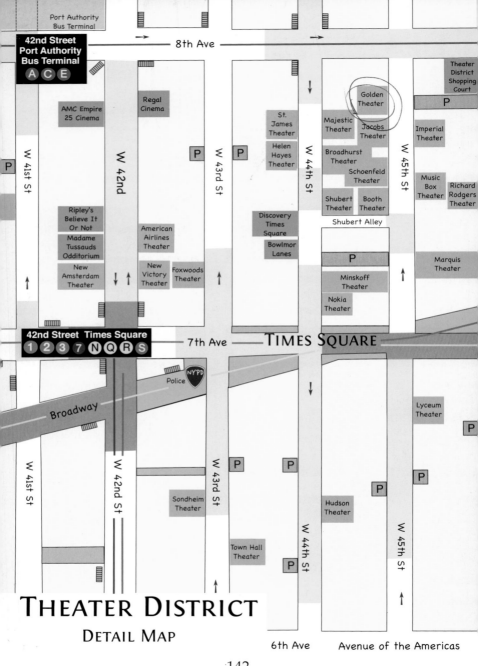

THEATER DISTRICT

DETAIL MAP

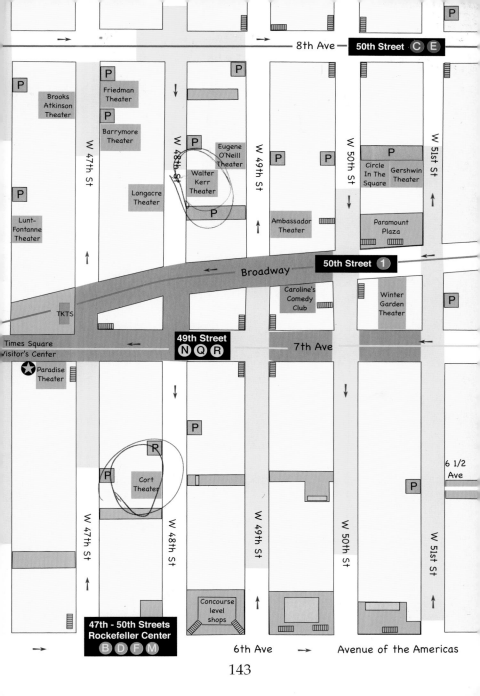

8th Ave

50th Street **C** **E**

P

P

Brooks
Atkinson
Theater

P

Friedman
Theater

P

P

Barrymore
Theater

W 47th St

W 48th St

P

Eugene
O'Neill
Theater

Walter
Kerr
Theater

Longacre
Theater

P

Lunt-
Fontanne
Theater

W 49th St

P

Ambassador
Theater

P

W 50th St

Circle
In The
Square

Gershwin
Theater

W 51st St

Paramount
Plaza

50th Street **1**

Broadway

TKTS

Caroline's
Comedy
Club

Winter
Garden
Theater

P

Times Square
Visitor's Center

49th Street
N **Q** **R**

7th Ave

Paradise
Theater

P

P

R

Cort
Theater

W 47th St

W 48th St

W 49th St

W 50th St

6 1/2
Ave

P

W 51st St

47th - 50th Streets
Rockefeller Center
B **D** **F** **M**

Concourse
level
shops

6th Ave

Avenue of the Americas

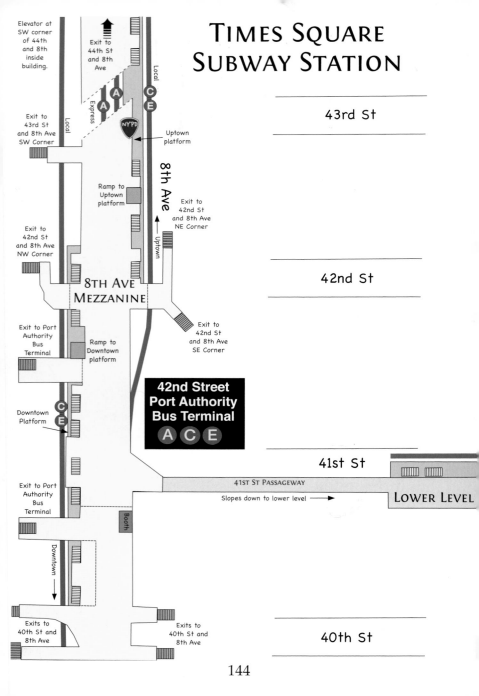

TIMES SQUARE
SUBWAY STATION

Elevator at SW corner of 44th and 8th inside building.

Exit to 44th St and 8th Ave

Exit to 43rd St and 8th Ave SW Corner

43rd St

Uptown platform

8th Ave

Ramp to Uptown platform

Uptown

Exit to 42nd St and 8th Ave NE Corner

Exit to 42nd St and 8th Ave NW Corner

42nd St

8TH AVE MEZZANINE

Exit to Port Authority Bus Terminal

Ramp to Downtown platform

Exit to 42nd St and 8th Ave SE Corner

42nd Street Port Authority Bus Terminal
A C E

Downtown Platform

41st St

Exit to Port Authority Bus Terminal

41ST ST PASSAGEWAY

Booth

Slopes down to lower level ⟶

LOWER LEVEL

Downtown

Exits to 40th St and 8th Ave

Exits to 40th St and 8th Ave

40th St

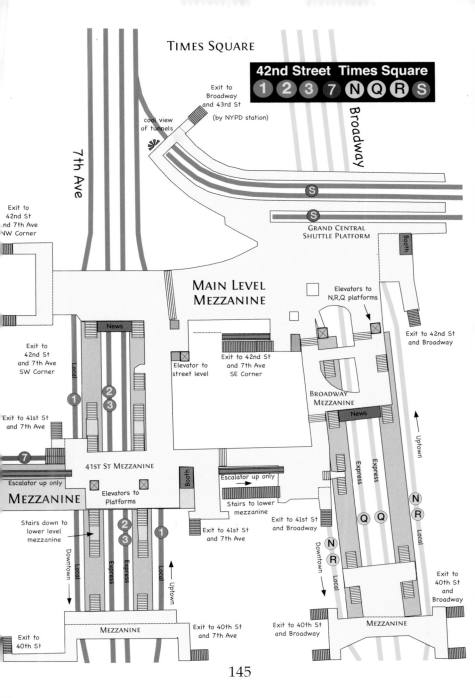

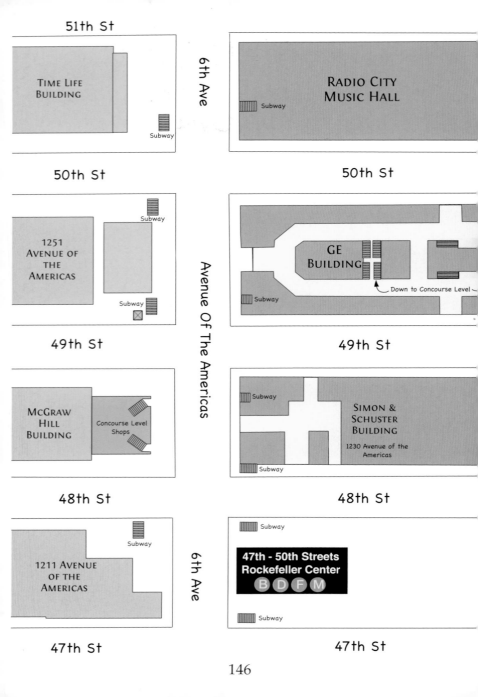

50th St

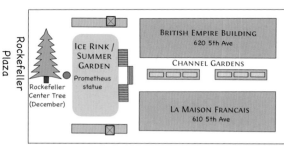

49th St

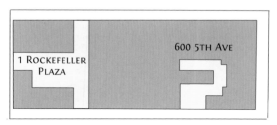

48th St

5th Ave

ROCKEFELLER CENTER
STREET LEVEL

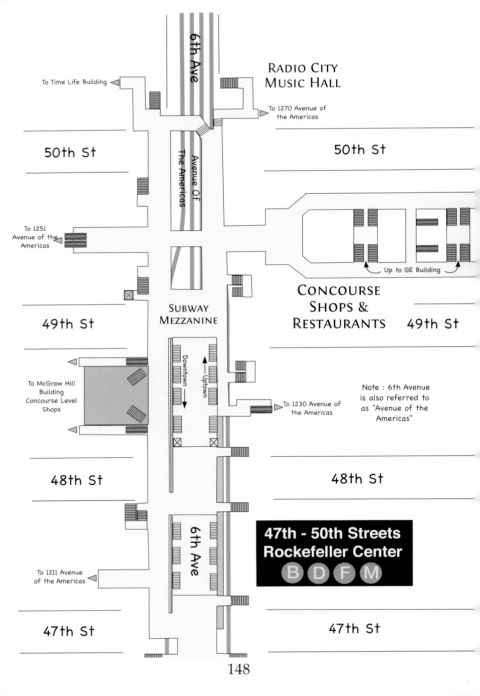

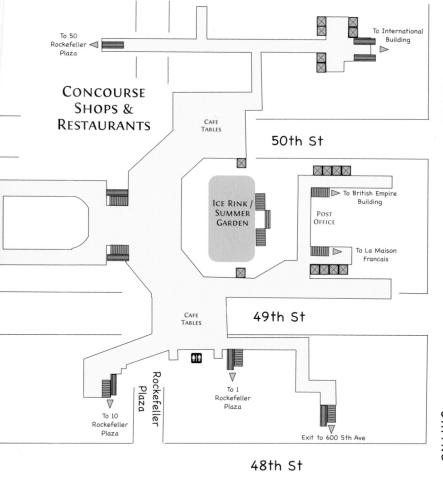

To 50
Rockefeller
Plaza

To International
Building

5th Ave

CONCOURSE
SHOPS &
RESTAURANTS

CAFE
TABLES

50th St

ICE RINK /
SUMMER
GARDEN

To British Empire
Building

POST
OFFICE

To La Maison
Francais

CAFE
TABLES

49th St

Rockefeller
Plaza

To 1
Rockefeller
Plaza

To 10
Rockefeller
Plaza

Exit to 600 5th Ave

5th Ave

48th St

ROCKEFELLER CENTER
LOWER CONCOURSE
& SUBWAY

MIDTOWN EAST   MAP 22

Abundant in famous buildings and architecture, the vast expanse of Midtown Manhattan stretches eastward beyond Park Avenue, eventually reaching the East River at the United Nations complex.

Grand Central Terminal

Serving over 750,000 people each day, Grand Central is by far the largest train station in the world. 67 tracks and 44 platforms are stacked on two levels and are completely underground, lying beneath several Park Avenue blocks. Even if you are not traveling by train, the interior of the beautiful 1913 terminal building is worth visiting. The main concourse features an immense ceiling mural of the heavens, complete with illuminated stars and astrological figures. It is also home to many retail stores and a dining concourse, the cornerstone of which is the famous Oyster Bar, now in operation for over 100 years. In addition to the shops and restaurants, you can also find a gourmet food market and an annex of the New York Transit Museum (the main museum is in Brooklyn and is definitely worth seeing). The New York Subway can be accessed directly from inside the terminal and includes a shuttle train that runs directly to Times Square. See detail map of Grand Central Terminal on pp. 160-161.

Grand Central Terminal & Met Life Building

 Met Life Building

Directly above Grand Central is the massive Met Life Building. Completed in 1963, it suffered initial unpopularity because of its huge scale and the way it dwarfed the historic buildings around it. When it opened, it was the largest commercial office space in the world.

Helmsley Building

Just north of Grand Central is the ornate Helmsley Building. Originally called the New York Central Building, it was built to house the headquarters and offices of the New York Central Railroad in 1929. Conceived to be a visual termination point for the railroad, the building can be seen from far north on Park Avenue.

 Chrysler Building

At the corner of 42nd Street and Lexington Avenue is the iconic Chrysler Building. An art deco masterpiece, it was the tallest building in the world for a short time after it opened in 1930. It lost that title when the Empire State Building was completed in 1931.

 St. Patrick's Cathedral

Across from Rockefeller Center on the east side of 5th Avenue at 51st Street is St. Patrick's Cathedral, New York's most famous Catholic church. The Neo-Gothic masterpiece was completed in 1879, after being under construction for twenty six years. When the cornerstone was laid in 1853, much of the public thought it was folly to build a church so far outside of the city in what they considered "the wilderness". Tours of the cathedral are available free of charge. St. Patrick's has a gift shop on 51st Street, as well as a smaller shop inside at the back of the cathedral.

Marilyn Monroe Subway Grate

Fans of Marilyn Monroe will want to pay homage to the subway grate at the northwest corner of 52nd Street and Lexington Avenue. This is the location of the famous scene in the 1955 film "Seven Year Itch", where Marilyn's dress gets blown up by the breeze as the trains go by. Filmed on September 15, 1954, thousands of people lined up behind barricades to witness the scene.

  Waldorf Astoria

This art-deco landmark is one of New York's oldest and most luxurious hotels. There are several restaurants on site. In the basement of the Waldorf is a "secret" subway track and platform that is connected to Grand Central Station. According to legend, President Franklin D. Roosevelt would use this way to enter the hotel, in order to hide the fact that he was in a wheelchair. This area is not open to the public.

 Park Avenue Plaza

A public atrium at 55 East 52nd Street features fountains, seating, rest rooms, seasonal plantings and trees.

  805 Atrium

Considered a "secret" by many, this indoor plaza features several restaurants and public seating. If you are lucky, you may even hear a piano player setting a relaxing mood during lunch time.

Madison Avenue

Manhattan's premiere shopping street, Madison Avenue is dominated by high end retail shops that continue northward for many blocks, far into the Upper East Side. The lower section between 43rd Street and 48th Street is devoted almost exclusively to men's fashions.

Grand Central Terminal Information Booth Clock

Did You Know?

The faces of the clock above the information booth in Grand Central Terminal are made of opal and are estimated to be worth between ten and twenty million dollars.

Turtle Bay MAP 22

In the early part of the 20th century, Turtle Bay was a grimy industrial neighborhood. With the construction of the United Nations, the neighborhood quickly transformed, as tenements and factories were torn down and replaced by brownstones. Today the area is an upscale residential neighborhood and home to the offices of many diplomats and dignitaries.

 United Nations

The United Nations is an international organization dedicated to establishing international law, human rights, development and peace between all nations. Visitors can take guided tours of the complex and visit the Security Council Chamber, Trusteeship Council Chamber, and the Economic and Social Council Chamber. Also open to the public is a visitor center, library and gift shop.

 Japan Society

Dedicated to the art and culture of Japan. Features indoor gardens, a theater, art gallery, and library.

 Greenacre Park

This tiny park is a peaceful oasis in the middle of the city. It features a waterfall, gardens, and abundant seating.

Dag Hammarskjold Plaza

Just to the west of the United Nations complex is Dag Hammarskjold Plaza, named for a former Secretary General of the United Nations. Six fountains create an atmosphere of peace. The plaza has long been known as a site for public demonstrations regarding world events. Across 1st Avenue stands "Good Defeats Evil", a large statue of Saint George spearing a dragon made from former Soviet and U.S. ballistic missiles.

 Ford Foundation Building

At the far eastern end of 42nd Street, The Ford Foundation Building raised the bar for indoor public spaces with its spectacular multi-story indoor gardens.

"Good Defeats Evil"

The United Nations Building

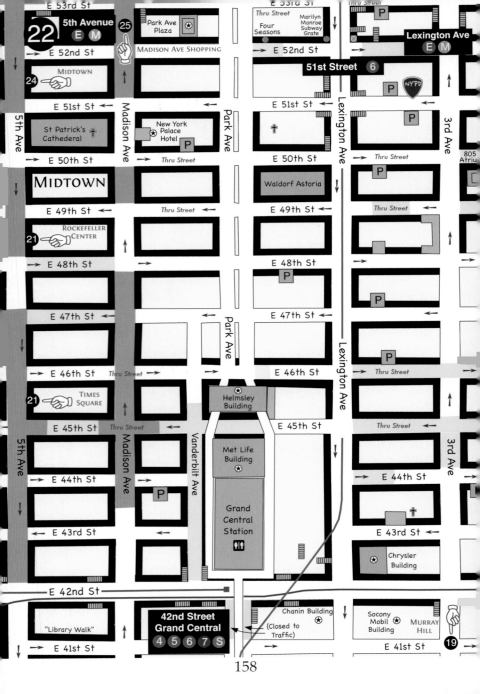

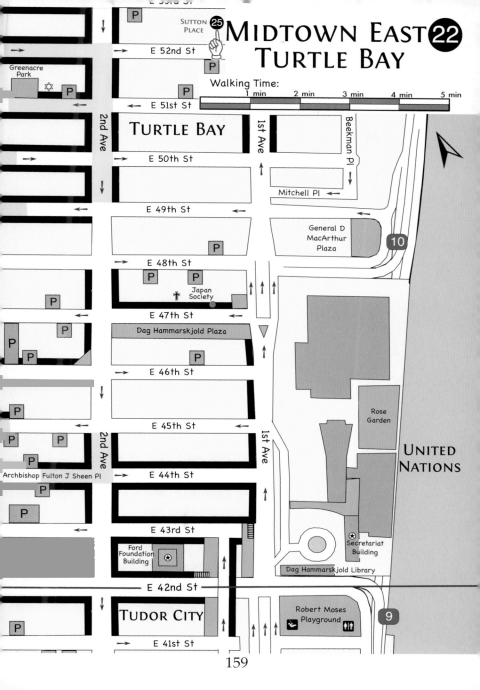

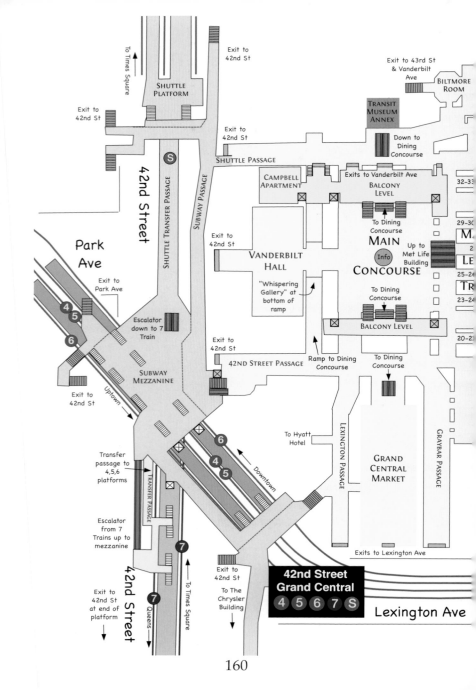

To Times Square

Exit to 42nd St

Exit to 43rd St & Vanderbilt Ave

BILTMORE ROOM

TRANSIT MUSEUM ANNEX

Exit to 42nd St

SHUTTLE PLATFORM

Down to Dining Concourse

Exit to 42nd St

Exits to Vanderbilt Ave

32-33

SHUTTLE PASSAGE

BALCONY LEVEL

29-30

CAMPBELL APARTMENT

SHUTTLE TRANSFER PASSAGE

SUBWAY PASSAGE

To Dining Concourse

M

2

LE

MAIN

Up to Met Life Building

42nd Street

Exit to 42nd St

VANDERBILT HALL

CONCOURSE

Info

25-26

TR

23-24

Park Ave

"Whispering Gallery" at bottom of ramp

To Dining Concourse

Exit to Park Ave

BALCONY LEVEL

20-21

4 5

Escalator down to 7 Train

6

Exit to 42nd St

42ND STREET PASSAGE

Ramp to Dining Concourse

To Dining Concourse

SUBWAY MEZZANINE

Exit to 42nd St

Uptown

6

To Hyatt Hotel

LEXINGTON PASSAGE

GRAND CENTRAL MARKET

GRAYBAR PASSAGE

Transfer passage to 4,5,6 platforms

TRANSFER PASSAGE

4 5

Downtown

Escalator from 7 Trains up to mezzanine

7

Exits to Lexington Ave

Exit to 42nd St at end of platform

42nd Street

7

Queens

To Times Square

Exit to 42nd St

To The Chrysler Building

42nd Street Grand Central
4 5 6 7 S

Lexington Ave

160

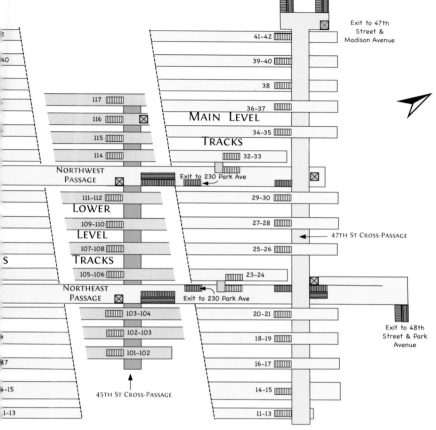

Exit to 47th
Street &
Madison Avenue

41–42

39–40

38

117

116

36–37

MAIN LEVEL

115

34–35

TRACKS

114

32–33

NORTHWEST
PASSAGE

Exit to 230 Park Ave

111–112

29–30

LOWER

109–110

27–28

LEVEL

107–108

25–26

47TH ST CROSS-PASSAGE

TRACKS

105–106

23–24

NORTHEAST
PASSAGE

Exit to 230 Park Ave

103–104

20–21

102–103

18–19

Exit to 48th
Street & Park
Avenue

101–102

16–17

14–15

45TH ST CROSS-PASSAGE

11–13

Metro-North Railroad

GRAND CENTRAL TERMINAL

While not shown on this map, beneath the Main Concourse is the massive Dining Concourse which is accessed via many escalators, ramps, and stairways. Here you can find all manner of fast food and cafes, as well as the famous Oyster Bar. For more upscale fare, explore the balconies overlooking the Main Concourse. There are several excellent restaurants with views of all the action below. Most exclusive of all is the Campbell Apartment. This dim 1920s style bar was once the office of real estate tycoon John W Campbell. Restored to its former glory, it exudes opulence, wealth, power, and elegance...the very spirit of Grand Central Terminal.

Midtown   Map 24

This is the core of the Big Apple, and is by far the busiest commercial district in the United States. Featuring nearly endless shopping, dining, and entertainment opportunities, Midtown Manhattan has it all.

 Alwyn Court

On the corner of 58th Street are the Alwyn Court Apartments. The 1909 French Renaissance style building is one of the most beautiful and ornate in all of Manhattan.

French Renaissance Architecture on Alwyn Court

Carnegie Hall

Built in 1891, Carnegie Hall has long been known as one of New York City's most prestigious theaters, featuring orchestral concerts, pop and jazz performances, and classical recitals. Tours of the theater are available.

 Carnegie Deli

This landmark deli opened in 1937 and has been serving its famous giant sandwiches ever since. The deli's motto is: "If you can finish your meal, we've done something wrong!"

 Museum of Modern Art

The Museum of Modern Art was established in 1929 and, not surprisingly, features Modernist art. Visit the Terrace 5 restaurant in the museum for outdoor rooftop dining in season.

 Paley Center for Media

Formerly known as the Museum of Television and Radio, the Paley Center has now expanded to include newer broadcast technologies such as the Internet. The center contains a library of over 120,000 TV shows, commercials, and radio shows, which can be viewed and heard by visitors at private consoles.

Trump Tower Atrium

This large restaurant and retail atrium features a multi-story waterfall and adjoins a bright glass-enclosed bamboo forest on the Madison Avenue side. There are rest rooms on the lower level.

  Time Warner Center

Adjacent to Columbus Circle is the massive Time Warner Center. Completed in 2003, it houses a multi-story upscale shopping mall, a Whole Foods store, a 1,200-seat theater, and several restaurants. Like the Wall Street Bull, the huge statues of a man and woman in the lobby are anatomically correct, and from the looks of it, endure quite a bit of fondling from visitors.

 Fifth & Madison Avenues

New York's top shopping district is centered here along 5th and Madison Avenues. All the big designers and prestige brands have stores here. Famous retail addresses include Tiffany's, Henri Bendel, Bergdorf Goodman, and Barneys. Wear good walking shoes and bring your credit cards, because the upscale shops, boutiques, and galleries just go on and on.

 FAO Schwartz

The famous FAO Schwartz store is not only the oldest toy store in the United States, it has become a beloved tourist destination.

6th 1/2 Avenue

If you walk the blocks between 6th and 7th Avenues in the 50's, you'll come upon the curious 6th ½ Avenue. For long a secret known only to Midtown office workers, the interconnected mid-block route of lobbies, atriums, passageways and parks now has an official designation.

6th 1/2 Avenue

SUTTON PLACE   MAP 25

Sutton Place has been a fashionable East Side neighborhood since the 1920s. Referring to the street of the same
name (actually a disconnected portion of Avenue A) and
the surrounding blocks, Sutton Place is home to many
celebrities and prominent New Yorkers.

 Central Synagogue

This national landmark synagogue was built in 1872 and
is the oldest synagogue in continuous use in the city. It
is open to the public Tuesdays and Wednesdays from
12:00-2:00 pm for meditation and tours.

 Mount Vernon Hotel Museum & Garden

Built in 1799 as a carriage house, the building was converted into a hotel in 1826 and was known in the 19th
century as a fashionable country resort. It was turned
into a museum in 1939. Also on the grounds are seasonal gardens and a gift shop.

   Citigroup Center

This iconic slant-roof building is not only a signature
element of New York's skyline, it also features a three
story public atrium that is home to several shops and
restaurants.

Design District

The blocks around the Roosevelt Island Tramway terminal are known as the Design District. Here you will find home stores, interior design firms, and antique shops.

 Manhattan Arts & Antique Center

One of the oldest antique emporiums in the city, the Manhattan Arts and Antique Center features over 100 galleries selling antique furniture, rugs, and paintings, as well as many other design accessories.

 Madison Avenue

New York City's high-end shopping district can be found on this part of Madison Avenue. This prestigious stretch of stores and boutiques has most of the world's luxury brands represented. Starting in Midtown at around 43rd Street, this shopping district extends for thirty blocks to around 73rd Street. Smaller boutique shops and galleries dominate the northern end, while the lower section features well known prestige designers.

 Bloomingdales

Covering an entire city block, the Bloomingdales flag-ship store has been a major shopping destination since 1886, and is another great rainy day diversion. You can enter Bloomingdales directly from the uptown local platform of the Lexington Avenue subway (4,5,6).

Queensboro Bridge & Roosevelt Island Tramway

Dominating the landscape of the neighborhood is the Queensboro Bridge, also known as the 59th Street Bridge, or its official designation, The Ed Koch Queensboro Bridge. It connects Manhattan with Long Island City, Queens. Just to the north of the span is the Roosevelt Island Tramway. This aerial tram carries passengers high above the East River and connects Manhattan with Roosevelt Island, which is situated in the middle of the river. Now almost completely residential, Roosevelt Island was previously known as Welfare Island and was home to several hospitals, a penitentiary, and a lunatic asylum. The tramway can be accessed via a standard metrocard and leaves every 15 minutes. The crossing takes about 4 minutes and offers great views of Manhattan and Queens.

Roosevelt Island tram

Queensboro Bridge

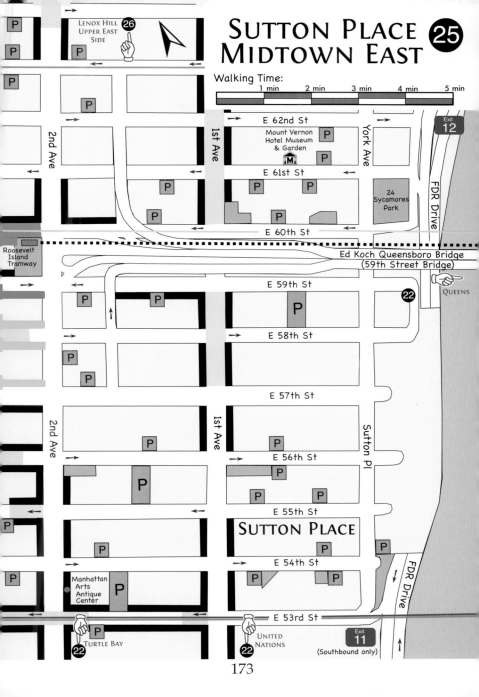

Lenox Hill Upper East Side 26

Walking Time:

| | 1 min | 2 min | 3 min | 4 min | 5 min |

P

2nd Ave

1st Ave

E 62nd St

Mount Vernon Hotel Museum & Garden

York Ave

Exit 12

E 61st St

24 Sycamores Park

FDR Drive

E 60th St

Roosevelt Island Tramway

Ed Koch Queensboro Bridge (59th Street Bridge)

QUEENS

E 59th St

P

22

E 58th St

E 57th St

1st Ave

2nd Ave

Sutton Pl

E 56th St

P

E 55th St

SUTTON PLACE

E 54th St

FDR Drive

Manhattan Arts Antique Center

P

E 53rd St

Exit 11

22 TURTLE BAY

22 UNITED NATIONS

(Southbound only)

Upper East Side

Comprised of the Lenox Hill, Yorkville, and Carnegie Hill neighborhoods, this whole area east of Central Park is generally referred to as the Upper East Side. This part of Manhattan has long been synonymous with upper class New York society, wealth, and luxury living. Fifth Avenue is known as "Museum Mile" in this area because of the many museums that are located along the east side of the park.

Lenox Hill   Map 26

The southernmost part of the Upper East Side is known as Lenox Hill, and was named after the thirty-acre farm belonging to Scottish merchant Robert Lenox. The original farmhouse once stood on the hill that rises around Madison and East 70th Street.

 Frick Collection

The Frick Collection opened in 1935 in the former Henry Clay Frick house. Located at 5th Avenue and 70th Street, this collection features old master paintings, furniture, rugs and sculpture.

 Madison Avenue

Upscale designer boutiques and luxury brand stores line Madison Avenue from Midtown to around East 72nd Street.

Third & Lexington Avenues

For a less intense (and less-expensive) shopping experience, you'll find popular mid-level brand stores along Third Avenue, while Lexington Avenue is home to many smaller specialty shops.

Frick Museum

Did You Know?

The Lexington Avenue subway (4,5,6) is the most crowded in the city. Daily ridership on this one line exceeds that of the entire Washington, D.C. Metro. In order to ease the congestion, New York City's newest subway is being built beneath Second Avenue. This long-awaited line has been on and off the drawing board since 1929, and will finally give riders on the Upper East Side another option to get downtown. The line is expected to open in phases, starting in late 2016.

YORKVILLE   MAP 27

The Upper East Side between East 79th Street and East
86th Street is known as Yorkville. For much of the 20th
century it was home to a large German, Hungarian,
and Czechoslovakian population. East 86th Street was
known as German Broadway, and 2nd Avenue between
80th and 86th Streets was known as Little Hungary. The
area was often referred to as "Little Bohemia". Today
Yorkville, like most of the Upper East Side, is an upper
class residential neighborhood and has lost much of
its ethnic feel. If you look carefully however, you can
still find a few holdouts from the earlier era in the form
of German and Hungarian restaurants, shops, and
churches.

 American Irish Historical Society

Across from the Metropolitan Museum Of Art, the
American Irish Historical Society celebrates Irish culture
through lectures, concerts, and art exhibits.

 New York Society Library

The New York Society Library on 79th Street is New
York's oldest cultural institution. Founded in 1754, it
has been housed in the present building since 1937. The
NYSL served as the city's library until the New York
Public Library was established in 1895.

The Metropolitan Museum of Art

The largest art museum in the United States, the Met houses an immense collection of paintings and sculptures from around the world. The museum also has permanent displays of jewelry, musical instruments, photographs, clothing, and armor & weapons. Opened in 1872, the building has over two million square feet of exhibition space, and features both permanent collections as well as traveling exhibitions throughout the year. The rooftop garden features a cafe and bar, and provides a bird's eye view of Central Park.

The Metropolitan Museum of Art

 ## Whitney Museum of American Art

The Whitney Museum focuses on 20th and 21st century American art, with an emphasis on living artists. Originally housed in a space in Greenwich Village, the museum moved to its present location on Madison Avenue at 75th Street in 1966. A new building is being built in the Meatpacking District and is slated for completion in 2015.

upper east side

Second & Third Avenues

When the Second Avenue subway opens, this area will be more accessible, but for now you'll have to walk or take a cab to this busy Upper East Side restaurant district. Both Second and Third Avenues offer lots of choices for dining and nightlife.

 East 86th Street

Popular mid-level brand retail can be found along E. 86th Street, between Park and Second Avenues.

 Madison Avenue

The luxury retail stores continue here in the form of specialty shops, designer boutiques and galleries.

 Third Avenue

You'll find plenty of mid-level brand retail stores and restaurants on Third Avenue below E. 78th Street.

Did You Know?

Records show that George Washington himself failed to return two books to the New York Society Library that were due in 1789. While the library is willing to waive the fine (which is now over $300,000), it is still seeking the return of the books.

Yorkville

CARNEGIE HILL   MAP 28

Carnegie Hill is the northernmost section of the Upper East Side. The neighborhood is named after Andrew Carnegie, an American industrialist who amassed a fortune in the steel industry and then became a major philanthropist. The traditional border between Carnegie Hill and Spanish Harlem to the north is East 96th Street, but in recent years the line has blurred, as more luxury housing is being developed in the high 90's. This is a classic example of "gentrification", an urban dynamic in which poor residents of a neighborhood are slowly displaced by rising rents and property values. This is a story that has played out all over Manhattan, but it is especially noticeable here, where the luxurious feel of the Upper East Side has been spreading steadily northward.

M Cooper Design Museum

The Cooper Design Museum is devoted exclusively to historic and contemporary design. It is a branch of the Smithsonian and is housed in the former Carnegie mansion on 5th Avenue at 91st Street.

M Guggenheim Museum

The Guggenheim is home to a collection of impressionist, early modern, and contemporary art. Designed by architect Frank Lloyd Wright, the building features a continuous spiral from the ground level to the skylight. Opened in 1959, the Guggenheim has become a neighborhood icon.

The Guggenheim Museum

 First, Second and Third Avenues

As inYorkville, most of the restaurants and nightclubs can be found on the eastern side of the neighborhood along First, Second, and Third Avenues.

 Madison Avenue

The luxury retail stores continue here in the form of designer boutiques and galleries.

26

27 METROPOLITAN MUSEUM OF ART

27 UPPER EAST SIDE YORKVILLE

E 74th St

E 73rd St

E 72nd St

E 71st St

E 70th St

E 69th St

E 68th st

E 67th St

E 66th St

E 65th St

5th Ave

Madison Ave

Park Ave

Lexington Ave

CENTRAL PARK
See Central Park map **33** for details

Museum Mile

The Frick Collection

P

P

P

68th Street / Hunter College **6**

P

Hunter College

5th Ave

Park Ave

Lexington Ave

To the West Side

MIDTOWN EAST

25

LENOX HILL
UPPER EAST SIDE

Walking Time:

| 1 min | 2 min | 3 min | 4 min | 5 min |

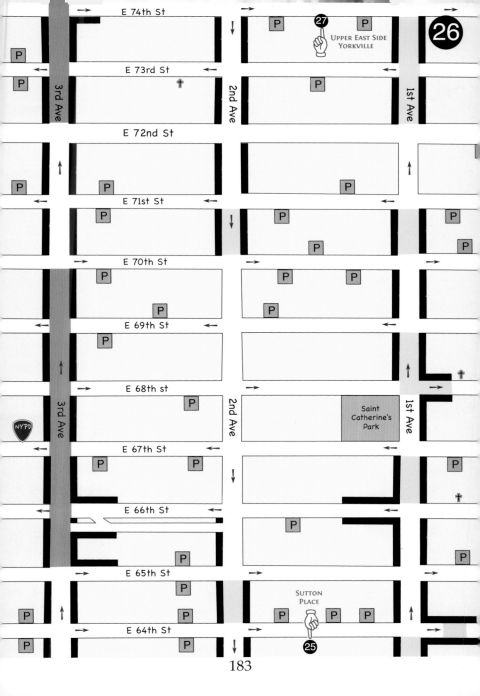

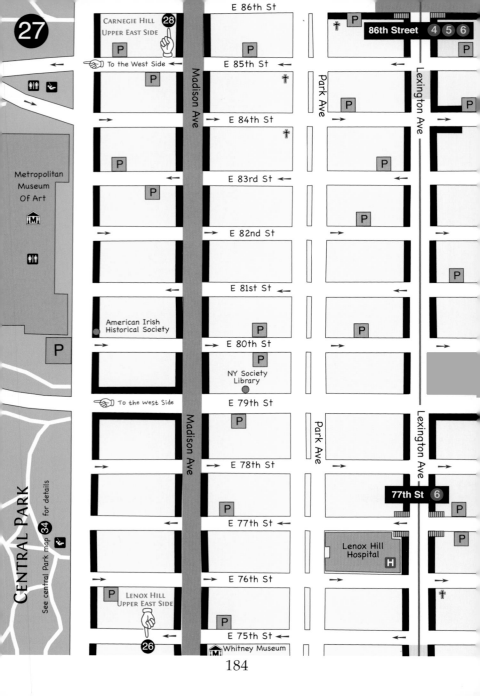

CARNEGIE HILL
UPPER EAST SIDE 28

To the West Side ←

E 86th St

E 85th St ←

E 84th St

E 83rd St ←

E 82nd St

E 81st St ←

E 80th St →

E 79th St

E 78th St

E 77th St ←

E 76th St

E 75th St ←

86th Street 4 5 6

Park Ave

Lexington Ave

Madison Ave

Metropolitan
Museum
Of Art

American Irish
Historical Society

NY Society
Library

To the West Side

CENTRAL PARK

See central Park map 34 for details

77th St 6

Lenox Hill
Hospital H

Lenox Hill
UPPER EAST SIDE

26

Whitney Museum

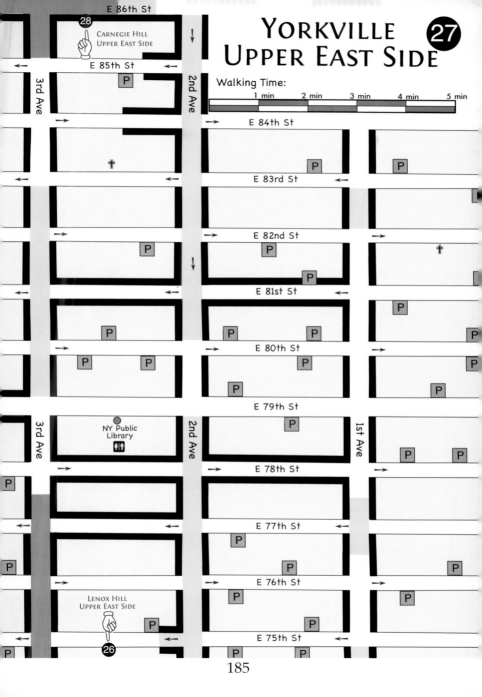

E 86th St

28

CARNEGIE HILL
UPPER EAST SIDE

E 85th St

3rd Ave

2nd Ave

P

Walking Time:

| 1 min | 2 min | 3 min | 4 min | 5 min |

E 84th St

E 83rd St

P

P

E 82nd St

P

P

E 81st St

P

P

P

P

E 80th St

P

P

P

P

P

E 79th St

P

3rd Ave

NY Public
Library

2nd Ave

1st Ave

P

P

E 78th St

P

P

E 77th St

P

P

P

P

E 76th St

LENOX HILL
UPPER EAST SIDE

P

P

P

P

E 75th St

P

P

P

26

CARNEGIE HILL
UPPER EAST SIDE

Walking Time: 1 min 2 min 3 min 4 min 5 min

E 97th St

E 96th St

E 95th St

E 94th St

E 93rd St

E 92nd St

E 91st St

E 90th St

E 89th St

E 88th St

E 87th St

E 86th St

2nd Ave

1st Ave

York Ave

FDR Drive

East River

Asphalt Green

(closed to traffic)

Ruppert Park

YORKVILLE
UPPER EAST SIDE

27

LINCOLN SQUARE MAP 29

Immortalized in the 1957 Broadway play "West Side Story", the area that is now Lincoln Square was previously a gritty working class neighborhood of run-down tenement buildings known as San Juan Hill. As part of an urban renewal project in the early 1960s, the neighborhood was razed to make way for a massive cultural complex which would come to be known as Lincoln Center.

 Lincoln Center for the Performing Arts

This sixteen-acre site includes the Metropolitan Opera House, Avery Fisher Hall, the David Koch Theater, the Juilliard School, Alice Tully Hall and the Lincoln Center Theater. Also on site is the New York Public Library of Performing Arts. The complex is home to the New York Philharmonic Orchestra, the New York City Ballet, the Metropolitan Opera, the Chamber Music Society and the Film Society Of Lincoln Center. There are cafes and fine dining establishments throughout Lincoln Center, along with several gift shops. The David Rubenstein Atrium is a public space that houses a visitor center, ticket office, cafe, and rest rooms. The visitor center also offers tours of the entire Lincoln Center complex.

American Folk Art Museum

Features 18th and 19th century folk art, including paintings, quilts, and sculptures. The museum's collection of quilts and other textiles is one of its most popular exhibits.

 Museum of Biblical Art

Around the corner from Columbus Circle, the Museum of Biblical Art showcases Christian and Jewish art inspired by the Bible and explores the influence of religion on art. Free admission.

 Riverside Park and Pier i

Originally part of the rail yards on the west side of Manhattan, Pier i was once used to transfer rail cars onto barges in the harbor. Now part of Riverside Park South, the pier features a cafe and hosts movies, activities, and events throughout the warmer months.

  Columbus Avenue

To the north of Lincoln Center, shopping and restaurants line Columbus Avenue, making for a pleasant walk through this upscale neighborhood. At 72nd Street, Verdi Square is the site of weekend markets and neighborhood events.

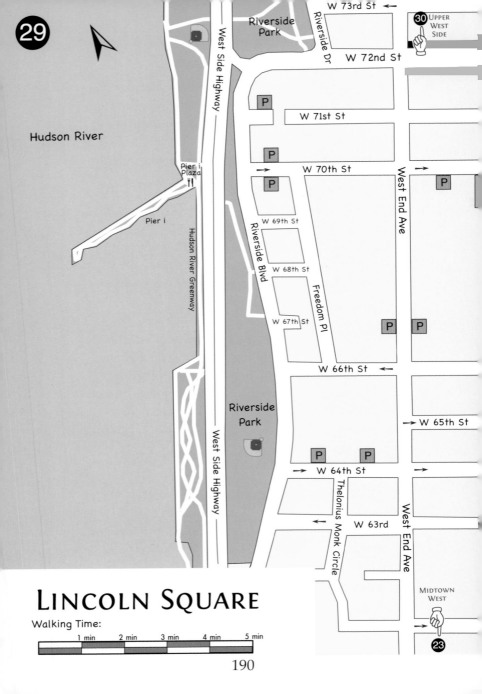

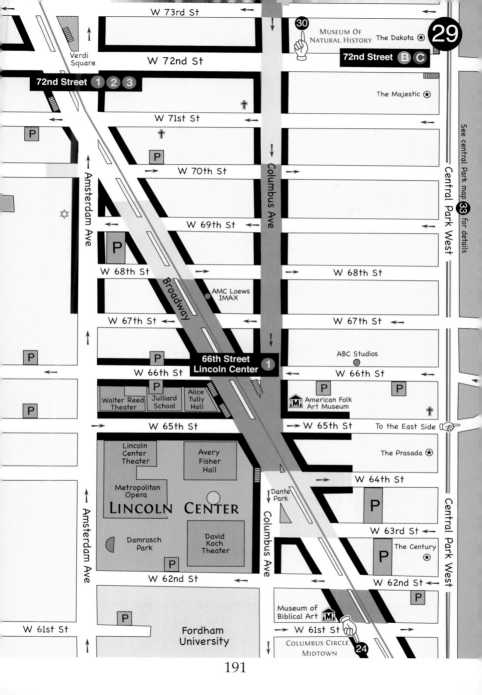

Upper West Side
Maps 30-32

The Upper West Side is an affluent residential neighbor-hood encompassing the broad area west of Central Park from around Lincoln Center northwards to 110th Street.

 Pommander Walk

The Upper West Side's "Secret Street", Pommander Walk is a gated residential courtyard just west of Broad-way between West 94th and 95th Streets. On either side of the walk are tiny tudor-style houses. It's not open to the public, but is worth a look through the gate if you are in the area.

 Children's Museum

Dedicated to nurturing new generations of creative global citizens, the Children's Museum features inter-active educational exhibits which focus on creativity, health, play, discovery and world cultures.

 New York Historical Society Museum & Library

One of the oldest research libraries in the U.S., the New York Historical Society has over two million documents and 900,000 photographs and prints. The museum features exhibits and programs relating to the history of New York City.

M American Museum of Natural History

The area's primary draw for visitors is the American Museum Of Natural History. Located across from Central Park at West 81st Street, it is one of the largest museums in the world. The museum has a collection of over 32 million items, a fraction of which are displayed in over 40 exhibition halls. The museum is dedicated to the natural history of the Earth itself and life upon it. Notable exhibits include Fossils, Dinosaurs, Gems & Minerals, Ocean Life, Astronomy, and various displays devoted to people and cultures from all over the world. In addition, the complex is home to the Hayden Planetarium. Built in 1935 and renovated in 2000, the star theater with its domed ceiling replicates a night sky as seen from earth. The theater also features space shows using high resolution full-dome video.

The American Museum of Natural History

Riverside Park

If you walk west towards the waterfront, you will come upon Riverside Park. This four-mile-long park sits between Riverside Drive and the Hudson River. What looks like a natural landscape is actually one of the engineering wonders of the city. Unknown to many, this landscape is actually built on top of a massive railroad tunnel that runs from around 123rd Street down to 39th Street. Constructed in the 1930s, the tunnel and the park were part of a West Side improvement project that included the Henry Hudson Parkway. In addition to its beautiful views of the river and New Jersey, the park features many recreational facilities and sports fields, including tennis, volleyball, and basketball courts. Free concerts and movies take place throughout the summer. The Hudson River Greenway connects the park to Riverside Park South and Hudson River Park, which goes all the way down to the southern tip of Manhattan at Battery Park. To the north, it connects to Riverbank State Park and Washington Park, making it part of a continuous waterfront right-of-way for pedestrians and cyclists.

West 79th Street Boat Basin

Operated by the Parks Department, the boat basin docks handle boats of all sizes, from canoes to large yachts. The marina features a waterfront cafe as well as a public kayak launch.

Bloomingdale District

Columbia University students frequent this pleasant restaurant district on Broadway between 104th and 108th Streets.

 Upper West Side Dining & Shopping

The Upper West Side is home to many restaurants, bars, specialty shops, and boutiques along Columbus and Amsterdam Avenues, as well as Broadway.

 Green Flea Market

A staple of the Upper West Side for over 25 years, the market features vendors selling a wide variety of goods, including antiques, crafts, collectibles, furniture, and clothing. Open Sundays year-round.

Did You Know?

The Riverside Park and Rail Tunnel Project cost over a hundred million dollars in the 1930s and was twice the scale of building the Hoover Dam.

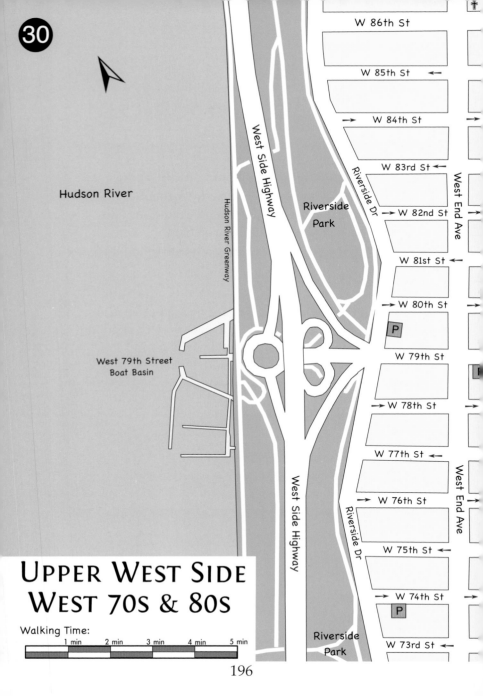

UPPER WEST SIDE
WEST 70S & 80S

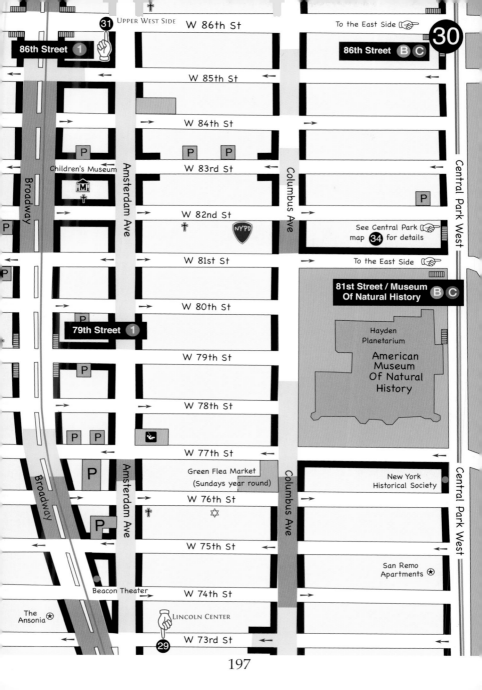

UPPER WEST SIDE   W 86th St   To the East Side 👉   **30**

31 👉

86th Street 1

86th Street B C

W 85th St

W 84th St

P

Children's Museum   W 83rd St   P   P

🏛   Columbus Ave   P

W 82nd St

†   NYPD

See Central Park 👉
map 34 for details

W 81st St   To the East Side 👉

81st Street / Museum B C
Of Natural History

W 80th St

P

79th Street 1   Hayden
Planetarium

W 79th St   American
Museum
Of Natural
History

P

W 78th St

P   P   ⛷

W 77th St

P   Green Flea Market   New York
(Sundays year round)   Historical Society

Amsterdam Ave   W 76th St   Columbus Ave

†   ✡

P   W 75th St

San Remo
Apartments ✴

Broadway   Beacon Theater   W 74th St

The
Ansonia ✴   👇 LINCOLN CENTER

29   W 73rd St

Broadway   Central Park West

197

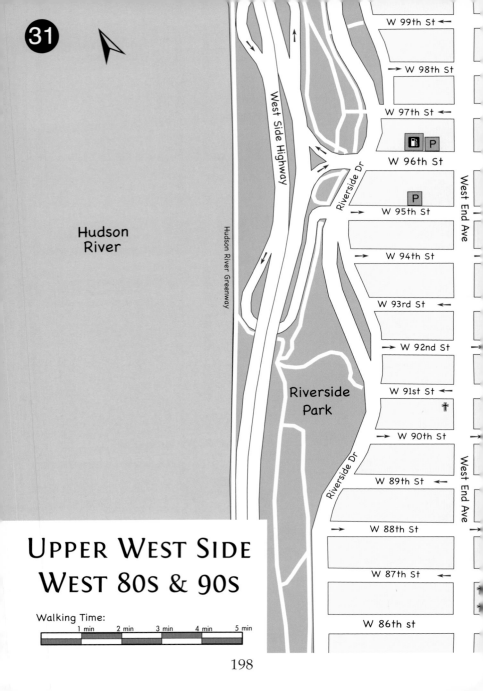

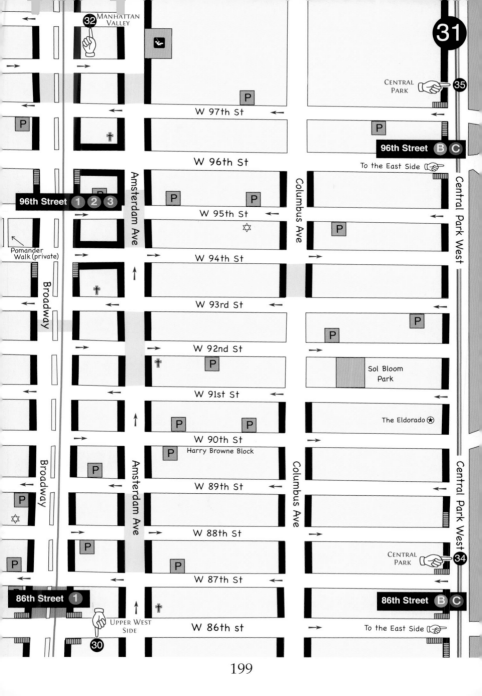

32 MANHATTAN VALLEY

31

CENTRAL PARK **35**

P

W 97th St

96th Street **B** **C**

W 96th St

To the East Side

96th Street **1** **2** **3**

Amsterdam Ave

P

P

Columbus Ave

W 95th St

P

Pomander Walk (private)

W 94th St

W 93rd St

P

P

W 92nd St

Sol Bloom Park

P

W 91st St

The Eldorado ★

Broadway

P

P

W 90th St

Harry Browne Block

P

W 89th St

Columbus Ave

P

W 88th St

P

CENTRAL PARK **34**

P

W 87th St

86th Street **1**

86th Street **B** **C**

UPPER WEST SIDE

W 86th st

To the East Side

30

199

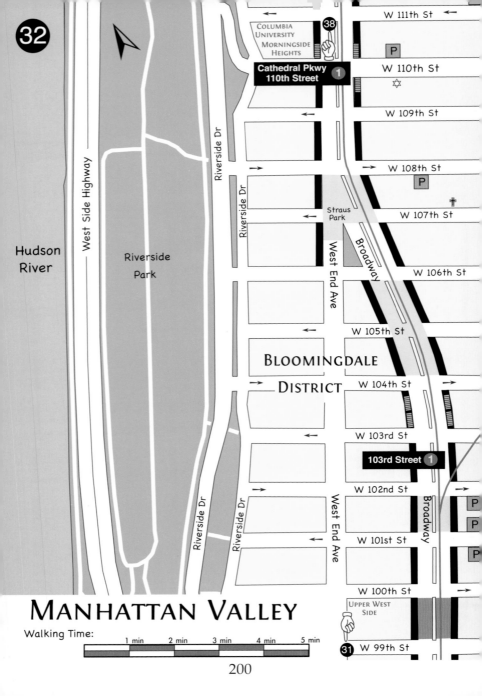

CENTRAL PARK Maps 33-35

While at first sight Central Park may seem to be a natural oasis of native flora, topography, and water features, it is actually quite the opposite. The park is the vision of landscape architects Frederick Law Olmstead and Calvert Vaux, and is an artistic landscape creation in its entirety. Each seemingly natural feature is a work of meticulous design, planned and placed as part of the larger vision of the park as a whole.

Under construction for over 20 years, Central Park was completed in 1873 and consists of 843 acres of lakes, ponds, woods, meadows, and gardens. Today the park is host to more than thirty million visitors each year, who come to enjoy the stunning landscapes and many amenities the park has to offer. In addition to the many natural wonders, Central Park is also home to a zoo, a pool, a carousel, and several outdoor theaters. Restaurants catering to all tastes and budgets can be found throughout the park. Also within the park's boundaries are a multitude of sports facilities, including a tennis center, croquet and bowling greens, volleyball courts and over twenty five baseball/softball fields. Children will be thrilled to find that Central Park is home to twenty-nine different playgrounds, all of which can be found along the outer edges of the park, close to the many entrances.

The following attractions can be found on Map 33 (Central Park South):

 Bow Bridge

Central Park's most famous bridge, the 60 foot span has been featured in many films and is considered one of the most iconic and romantic spots in the park.

Bow Bridge in Central Park

Children's Zoo

An interactive zoo for young children where they can pet and feed the animals.

 The Mall

The only formal design feature in the park, the Mall is lined with stately American Elm trees and leads to Bethesda Terrace. At the southern end of the Mall is the Literary Walk, which features statues of many famous literary figures.

 Naumburg Bandshell

Constructed in 1862 as a venue for classical music, today the Naumburg Bandshell hosts a summer concert series featuring a wide variety of musical styles.

 Summer Stage

An outdoor concert venue near the Rumsey Playfield, the Summer Stage offers free concerts throughout the summer months. Enter at 72nd Street and 5th Avenue.

 The Dairy

Central Park's main information center and gift shop. The Victorian gothic-style building was constructed in 1870.

The Arsenal

Built in 1848 to store ammunition and supplies for the New York State Militia, this building was here before the park was built. It now houses an art gallery.

 Carousel

Opened in 1871, the Central Park Carousel is one of the largest in the United States. It features 57 hand-carved horses and two chariots.

 Strawberry Fields

One of the most popular destinations in the park, the "Imagine" mosaic is a memorial to the late Beatle, John Lennon.

"Imagine" Mosaic at Strawberry Fields

Cherry Hill

This shady hillside overlooks the lake and Bow Bridge, and is a popular spot for lounging in the grass. Nearby is the Cherry Hill fountain with its distinctive glass Victorian-era lamps.

Cherry Hill Fountain

Grand Army Plaza

This plaza is where the Pulitzer Fountain and General Sherman statue are located. Horse and carriage rides through the park begin here.

 Delacorte Clock

Delacorte Clock is a musical clock which plays every half hour between 8:00 am and 5:00 pm. Songs change with the seasons.

 Central Park Zoo

Home to over 130 species of animals from around the world, the Central Park Zoo was New York's first zoo, opening in the 1860s. There are three exhibit areas - tropic, temperate, and polar. Popular animals on display include polar bears, sea lions, penguins, pandas, snow leopards, tamarins, and several species of birds.

 Wollman Rink

A public outdoor ice skating rink in the winter, Wollman Rink is also home to Victorian Gardens Amusement Park during the summer months. This small amusement park is geared towards children and features rides and games.

Bethesda Terrace and Fountain

Considered the heart of Central Park, the Bethesda Terrace and Fountain was named after a Biblical pool in Jerusalem that was believed to have healing waters. Overlooking the lake, the ornate terrace features intricate carvings and meticulously restored Victorian era architecture. The Bethesda Fountain is one of the largest in the city and features a sculpture known as the "Angel of the Waters".

 Conservatory Water

Designed in the spirit of model boat ponds in nineteenth century Paris, the Conservatory Water offers a place to sail model boats in modern day Central Park. Rentals are available at the Kerb Memorial Boathouse.

 The Ramble

A maze of woodland paths that cover 38 acres to the north of the lake, The Ramble contains many exotic trees and is a great area for bird watching. Certain areas can feel a little remote, so use caution and common sense if you are exploring alone or after dark.

  Loeb Boathouse

In addition to a restaurant and cafe, the Loeb Boathouse offers rowboat rentals, gondola rides, and bike rentals.

Tavern on the Green

One of New York City's most famous restaurants, the building also contains an information center and gift shop.

THE FOLLOWING ATTRACTIONS CAN BE FOUND ON MAP 34 (CENTRAL PARK CENTRAL):

 The Reservoir

Covering 106 acres, the Jacqueline Kennedy Onassis Reservoir holds over a billion gallons of water. It was built in 1862 to distribute clean drinking water to the city. Today it supplies water to many of the park's water features. The reservoir is surrounded by a popular 1.58 mile running track.

 The Obelisk

Commissioned by the Pharaoh Thutmosis III around 1450 BC, the Obelisk is the oldest man-made item in Central Park. Sometimes referred to as "Cleopatra's Needle", the obelisk is 71 feet high and weighs over 200 tons.

 Delacorte Theater

Known for its "Shakespeare In The Park" summer series, the Delacorte is an open air theater which overlooks Turtle Pond and Belvedere Castle.

central park

Shakespeare Garden

This beautiful four-acre garden is filled with plants and flowers mentioned in Shakespeare's plays.

 The Great Lawn

This 55-acre open space is the most famous lawn in the world, and is popular for picnicking, sunbathing, and casual games. Large concerts are occasionally held here.

 Swedish Cottage

This interesting building hosts marionette performances and is available to rent for children's birthday parties.

 Summit Rock

Summit Rock is the highest natural point in the park at 141.8 feet above sea level.

 Belvedere Castle

Built in 1865, this beautiful stone castle overlooks the Delacorte Theater, Great Lawn, and Turtle Pond. Vistas of the surrounding park can be seen from two rooftop parapets.

 Tennis Center

The Central Park Tennis Center features over 30 courts and offers private lessons for all skill levels.

Conservatory Garden

The only formal garden in Central Park, the Conservatory Garden features a wide array of plants and flowers that bloom throughout the year. It's worth visiting in the springtime to witness the wisteria in bloom on a massive iron pergola.

Wisteria Pergola in the Conservatory Garden

 North Meadow Recreation Area

Featuring basketball and handball courts, the rec center also rents out sport equipment to visitors.

central park

Discovery Center

The Discovery Center is a visitor's center on the northern edge of the park, offering many hands-on educational workshops throughout the year. Supplies for catch-and-release fishing in the Harlem Meer are available here.

Harlem Meer

 Wisteria Pergola

If you can't make it up to the Conservatory Gardens in the spring, check out the Wisteria Pergola near the Naumburg Bandshell. These fragrant purple flowers bloom profusely on a 130-foot-long pergola.

Lasker Pool and Rink

The Lasker Pool is free to the public from June to Labor Day, and offers free swim lessons for kids as well as adult lap swims. From November to March, the pool becomes the Lasker Ice Skating Rink.

 The Blockhouse

This small fort is the oldest structure in the park. It is the last remaining of three revolutionary-era forts constructed in upper Manhattan. It is not open to the public.

Evening in Central Park

central park

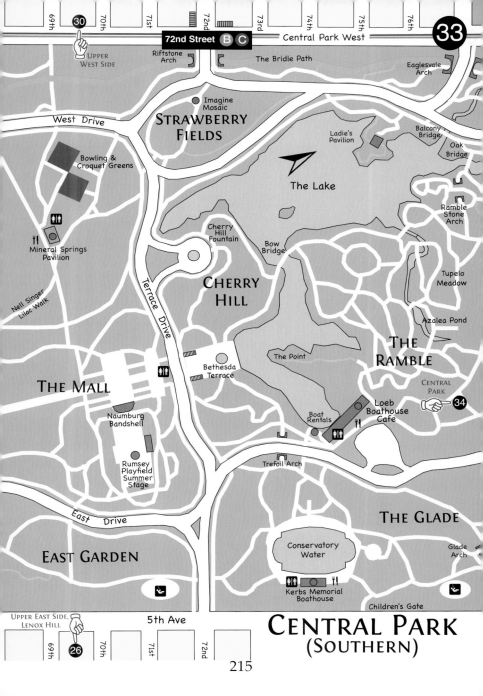

CENTRAL PARK
(SOUTHERN)

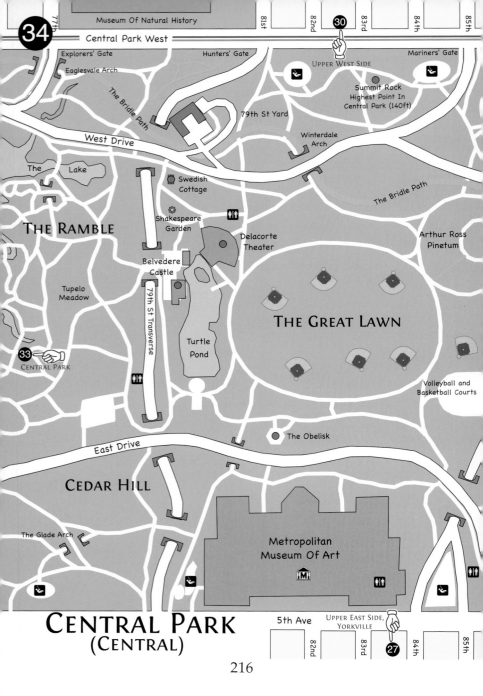

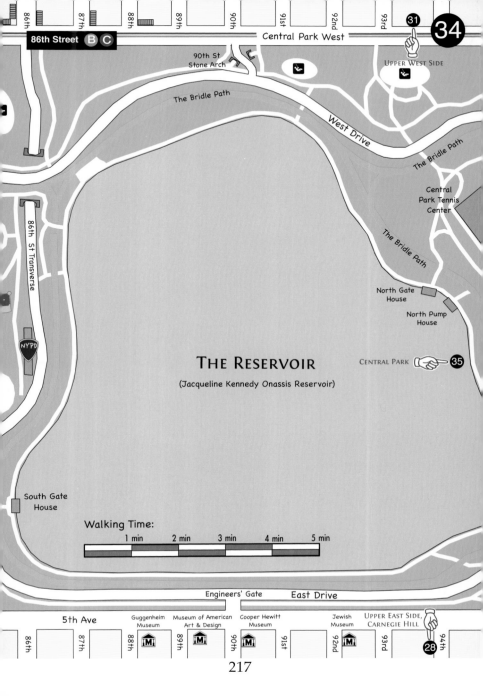

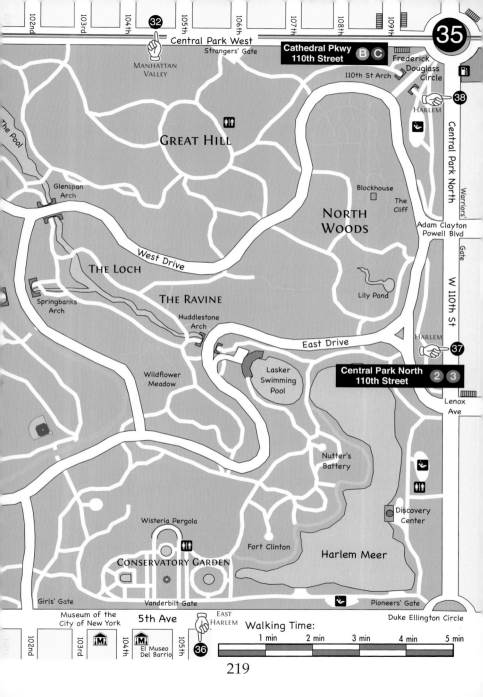

EAST HARLEM MAPS 36 & 37

East Harlem, also known as Spanish Harlem or El Barrio, is one of New York's largest Latino communities. Mainly residential and covering a large area of northeastern Manhattan, East Harlem has several commercial districts worth visiting. It's worth noting that some areas of these uptown neighborhoods may not be for everyone, so if you decide to explore, please use common sense and be aware of your surroundings. That said, the adventurous will find a rich cultural experience. Famous murals adorn buildings throughout the neighborhood, but the biggest and most popular is the "Spirit Of East Harlem", painted on an entire building facade at the corner of Lexington and 104th Street.

 El Museo Del Barrio
This museum was founded in 1969, when community parents, teachers, and activists demanded education for their children that acknowledged East Harlem's diverse cultural heritage. It is dedicated to Caribbean, Latino, and Latin American art.

 Museum of African Art
Opened in 1984, the Museum of African Art is dedicated to the art and culture of Africa. The museum also offers public programs that include lectures, film series, and hands-on workshops.

The "Spirit of East Harlem" mural

M **Museum of the City of New York**

Founded in 1923, the Museum of the City of New York celebrates the heritage, diversity, and perpetual transformation of New York City.

Lexington Avenue

A pleasant block of restaurants and bars can be found along Lexington between East 100th Street and East 101st Street.

  East 116th Street

East Harlem's primary business hub can be found along East 116th Street. It's lined with ethnic-themed shops, discount fashion retailers, Mexican restaurants, and fast food joints.

 Third Avenue

For discount shopping, cultural flavor, and impressive street murals, explore the commercial district that runs along Lexington and 3rd Avenue from 100th to 108th Streets. Discount variety and department stores are interspersed with specialty shops and fast food restaurants.

East Harlem mural

upper manhattan

HARLEM MAPS 37-39

North of Central Park, you will find the neighborhood of Harlem. It could be argued that Harlem is the epicenter of African-American culture in the western hemisphere. Plagued by drugs and crime for decades, the neighborhood has undergone an impressive transformation. With crime rates plummeting over 73% in the past two decades, Harlem has been reborn as a place of rich sensory experience and cultural significance.

 Malcolm Shabazz Harlem Market

This West African Bazaar features over 85 vendors selling traditional African crafts, clothing, music, jewelry, art, beauty products and souvenirs. Don't be afraid to haggle; its all part of the experience.

 Cotton Club

Famous for its southern cuisine and big band music, the Cotton Club hosts gospel brunch, swing dancing, and big band, jazz and Latin nights.

The Cotton Club

Apollo Theater

A neighborhood and cultural icon since it opened in 1934, the Apollo Theater is famous for helping launch the careers of many notable African-American artists. Ella Fitzgerald, Billie Holiday, James Brown, Diana Ross, Marvin Gaye, Stevie Wonder, and Jimi Hendrix are just a few of the musicians that got their start on the Apollo's famous stage.

The Apollo Theater

Manhattanville/ViVa

The area around the far western end of W. 125th Street was once the location of the waterfront village of Manhattanville. As the city expanded northward, the community became obsolete and was absorbed into the growing metropolis. Today the area is known as "ViVa" (**Vi**aduct **Va**lley), named for the large viaducts that cross the natural valley here. To avoid difficult grades, the subway (number 1 line) comes out above ground on one side of the valley, crosses it on a viaduct, and then disappears back underground on the other side. A small restaurant district has sprung up around the 125th Street elevated station.

125th Street elevated subway station

 Jazz Museum

Dedicated to the history of jazz music, the museum features many events, programs and exhibitions throughout the year.

 Studio Museum of Harlem

Founded in 1968, the museum exhibits works that have been influenced by black culture. Free on Sundays.

Marcus Garvey Park

Originally named Mount Morris Park, it was re-named for the African-American writer and naturalist Marcus Garvey. The park features a landmark fire watchtower, the sole survivor of eleven such towers that once stood throughout the city. The park itself dates to 1840 and was a natural location due to the rocky outcropping of Mount Morris, which blocked the northward path of 5th Avenue. The park also features an outdoor pool and an amphitheater, which hosts a summer concert series.

Le Petit Senegal

Known as Harlem's "Gold Coast", Frederick Douglass Boulevard (8th Avenue) is home to an expanding restaurant district as well as upscale housing. This colorful area, especially around 116th Street, is home to many West African immigrants.

Malcolm X Boulevard (Lenox Ave.)

Just to the north of West 125th Street is a pleasant restaurant district with plenty of al fresco seating in the warm months. Several of these restaurants are known for their gospel or jazz brunches on weekend mornings. Most famous is Sylvia's, known as the "Queen of Soul Food" since 1962.

West 125th Street

Harlem's main shopping and business district is along 125th Street. Here you will find locally-owned specialty shops mixed with mass market and bargain retail stores.

Did You Know?

If you visit 125th Street during non-business hours, you will be treated to a multitude of street murals painted on storefront security gates. These paintings of African-American themes are the work of Franco the Great, known locally as "the Picasso of Harlem".

Mural by Franco the Great

Morningside Heights
Map 38

Situated on a ridge high above the Hudson River,
Morningside Heights is Manhattan's academic quarter.
While the neighborhood is dominated by Columbia University, there are several smaller colleges, schools, and
seminaries in the area as well. Morningside Park creates
a natural separation between the "Academic Acropolis"
on the heights and the neighborhood of Harlem in the
valley to the east.

 Cathedral of Saint John the Divine

The largest cathedral in the world, the nave of Saint
John the Divine is longer than two football fields and is
home to the largest rose window in the United States.
Construction began in 1892, and although the cathedral
opened in 1941, it is still unfinished. Stonework continued into the 1990s, but as of this writing, no further
construction has been planned for the immediate future.
In addition to regularly scheduled religious services, the
cathedral hosts many events and programs throughout
the year. On the grounds is a "Biblical Garden" featuring plants and flowers mentioned in the Bible.

 Grant's Tomb

A national memorial to Civil War general and later
President Ulysses S. Grant, it is the largest mausoleum
in the United States. The building is maintained by the
National Park Service and is open to the public.

Columbia University

Founded in 1754, Columbia University is the oldest
college in New York. The campus is open to the public,
and there is a visitor's center at the Low Library. This
is the location of the famous "Low Steps" which is a
New York City landmark and a favorite gathering place
for Columbia students. In front of the library is "Alma
Mater", a statue of the Goddess Athena. Hidden in
the folds of her cloak is a tiny carved owl representing
spiritual wisdom. Legend has it that the first member of
each year's incoming class to find the owl will become
valedictorian. The Low Library and Saint Paul's Chapel
are both open to the public. All other buildings require a
Columbia University ID. Guided tours are available.

The "Low Steps" at Columbia University

Riverside Church

High on a ridge overlooking the Hudson River stands the magnificent Riverside Church. The bell tower is the tallest in the United States and houses a carillon – which consists of 74 bronze bells and includes the largest tuned bell in the world, weighing in at 20 tons.

Riverside Church

Morningside Park

Due to the severe nature of the topography in this part of Manhattan, it was deemed impractical to force the street grid upon the steep cliffs and different elevations in this area. The area was designated a park during the late nineteenth century, and construction was completed in 1895. The park features walking paths, sports fields, basketball courts, and an arboretum. One of the best ways to enjoy the park is from above - there is a wide sidewalk along Morningside Drive which has several cliff-top spots to take in the view.

 Dining in Morningside Heights

While the area is not a dining destination, there are a few restaurants in the area of Columbia University. Fans of the television sitcom "Seinfeld" will recognize Tom's Diner.

Did You Know?

The Revolutionary War Battle of Harlem Heights was fought here on September 16, 1776. George Washington's Continental Army clashed with the British in a wheat field that was located where Barnard College now stands. A plaque commemorating the battle can be found on Broadway between W. 117th and W. 118th Streets.

upper manhattan

36

38 HARLEM

W 114th St

W 113th St

37 HARLEM

Malcom X Blvd

5th Ave

Madison Ave

St Nicholas Ave

Adam Clayton Powell Jr. Blvd

7th Ave

W 112th St

Lenox Ave

P

P

W 111th St

**Central Park North
110th Street** ② ③

38 MORNINGSIDE HEIGHTS

W 110th St

Duke Ellington Circle

E 110th St

Museum of
African Art

E 109th St

E 108th St

Harlem Meer

E 107th St

"Graffiti
Hall of
Fame"
Mural

Lasker Rink
& Pool

E 106th St

P

West Drive

CENTRAL PARK

See Central Park map **35** for
details

P

E 105th St

El Museo
Del Barrio

Conservatory
Garden

5th Ave

E 104th St

Museum of
The City
of New York

East Drive

E 103rd St

E 102nd St

102nd St Cutoff

E 101st St

Museum Mile

Madison Ave

CARNEGIE HILL
UPPER EAST
SIDE

28

E 115th St

Park Ave

Lexington Ave

Walking Time:

| 1 min | 2 min | 3 min | 4 min | 5 min |

E 112th St

3rd Ave

2nd Ave

1st Ave

E 111th St

110th St 6

Tito Puente Way

E 110th St

E 109th St

EAST HARLEM

E 108th St

E 106th St

"Che Guevara & Albizu Campos" Mural

Lexington Ave

P

E 105th St

"Spirit of East Harlem" Mural

103rd St 6

E 104th St

3rd Ave

2nd Ave

1st Ave

E 103rd St

E 102nd St

Park Ave

NYPD

CARNEGIE HILL
UPPER EAST SIDE

E 101st St

28

E 100th St

HARLEM

37

Walking Time:

| 1 min | 2 min | 3 min | 4 min | 5 min |

Madison Ave

P

Jazz Museum

Lexington Ave

W 126th St ←

P

3rd Ave

W 125th St

Demolition Depot ●

P

P

MTA Metro North 125th St

125th Street ④ ⑤ ⑥

W 124th St →

Park Ave

Ode to
Picasso
mural ●

W 123rd St ←

P

W 122nd St →

W 121st St ←

W 120th St →

W 119th St ←

NYPD

W 118th St →

Lexington Ave

EAST

✝

HARLEM

P

W 117th St ←

Madison Ave

Urban
Garden
Center ●

116th Street ⑥

★

P

W 116th St

East Harlem, (Lower)

36

✝

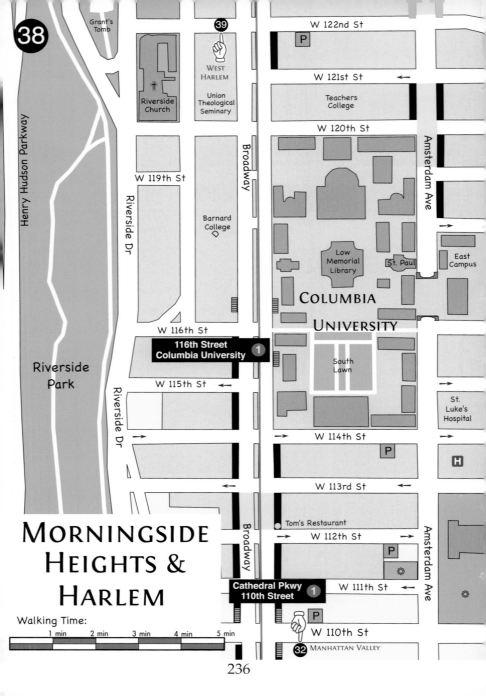

38

39

☝ HARLEM

W 122nd St

Harriet Tubman Square

W 121st St

W 120th St

HARLEM

W 119th St

W 118th St → St Nicholas Ave

W 117th St

P HARLEM ☞ **37**

W 116th St

116th Street **B** **C**

LITTLE SENEGAL

NY Public Library ●

W 115th St

W 114th St

W 113rd St

W 112th St

W 111th St

Cathedral Pkwy **B** **C**
110th Street

EAST HARLEM ☞ **36**

Frederick Douglass Circle

32 MANHATTAN VALLEY

W 110th St

CENTRAL PARK See map **35**

Morningside Dr

Manhattan Ave

8th Ave = Fredrick Douglass Blvd

7th Ave

Morningside
Park

8th Ave = Frederick Douglass Blvd

Manhattan Ave

Morningside Dr

Cathedral
of Saint
John The Divine

P

39 MANHATTANVILLE
WEST HARLEM, VIVA

Walking Time:

1 min	2 min	3 min	4 min	5 min

W 135th St

W 134th st

Hudson River

W 133rd St

W 132nd St

W 131st St

W 130st St

Henry Hudson Pkwy

Marginal St

Riverside Dr

West Harlem Piers

Hudson River Greenway

Broadway

Old Broadway

Amsterdam Ave

Cotton Club

St. Clair Pl

W 129th st

W 125th St

ViVa

125th Street 1

Tiemann Pl

Old Broadway

W 129th st

W 125th St

elevated subway

Riverside Dr

La Salle St

Claremont Ave

Broadway

Henry Hudson Pkwy

Hudson River Greenway

General Grant National Memorial

Amsterdam Ave

W 123rd St

Sakura Park

MORNINGSIDE HEIGHTS/ COLUMBIA UNIVERSITY

38

Riverside Dr

Riverside Cathedral

W 122nd St

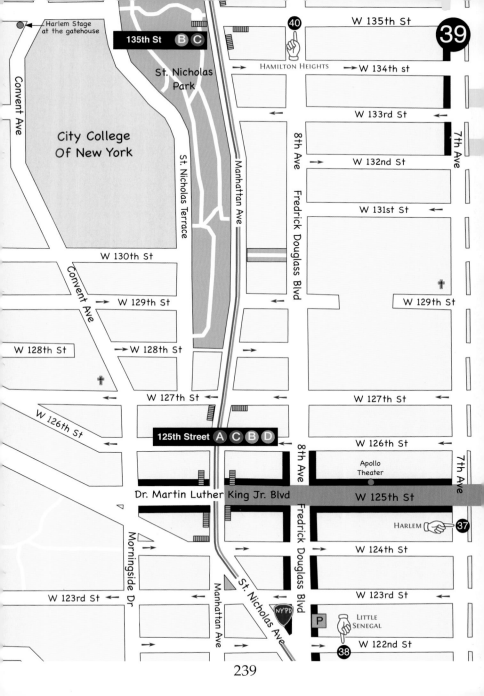

Hamilton Heights
Map 40

Historically, Hamilton Heights was an affluent African-American neighborhood and was often called Sugar Hill, referring to the "sweet life" of those that could afford to live there. Many famous names are associated with the area including Duke Ellington, Adam Clayton Powell Jr., Frankie Lymon, and Willie Mays.

 City College of New York

The centerpiece of Hamilton Heights is the beautiful City College Of New York. The gothic-style Shepard Hall towers over Saint Nicholas Park and can be seen for many blocks.

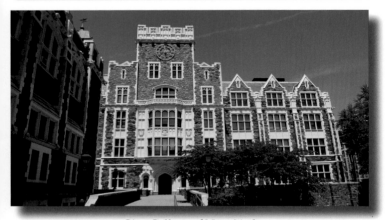

City College of New York

Abyssinian Baptist Church

On the border of Hamilton Heights and Harlem, the Abyssinian Baptist Church is one of the oldest Baptist churches in the United States. The congregation welcomes visitors for its 11:00 am service on Sundays. Please check their website for more information.

 Riverbank State Park

Situated on the Hudson waterfront, this 28-acre multi-level sports and recreation center is set high above the river. It features an Olympic-size pool, a skating rink, tennis, basketball, and handball courts, playgrounds, a running track, and football and soccer fields. The park is also home to a theater and a restaurant.

 Saint Nicholas Park

One of Harlem's largest parks, Saint Nicholas Park features walking paths, basketball courts, gardens and playgrounds. The very southern tip was once known as the "Point of Rocks" and was George Washington's position during the battle of Harlem Heights in the Revolutionary War.

 Jackie Robinson Park

Adjacent to the A,C,B,D Subway at 145th Street is the area's most popular park, featuring a pool and recreation center, a water play area, basketball courts and baseball fields. A band shell hosts music events throughout the summer months.

WASHINGTON HEIGHTS
MAPS 41 & 42

Above West 155th Street is Washington Heights. Largely populated by Dominicans, the area has a strong Latin feel and is often referred to as "Little Dominican Republic".

 Trinity Cemetery

Overlooking the Hudson River from Washington Heights, Trinity Cemetery is the final resting place of many famous New Yorkers and historic figures. In addition to its historic residents, it's worth visiting simply because it is one of Manhattan's most beautiful green spaces. There is a gate on West 153rd Street.

 Hispanic Society of America

This free museum and reference library is dedicated to the study of Hispanic art and culture.

Hispanic Society of America

Morris Jumel Mansion Museum

Built in 1765, the Morris Jumel Mansion is Manhattan's oldest surviving house. It served as a headquarters for George Washington during the revolution, and he later hosted dinner here for his cabinet in 1790. The mansion became a museum in 1904.

Morris Jumel Mansion Museum

Fort Washington Park

This waterfront park is home to New York City's most famous lighthouse. Immortalized in Hildegard Swift's children's book of the same name, the Little Red Lighthouse can be found on the bank of the Hudson River beneath the George Washington Bridge. Officially named "Jefferey's Hook Light", it was built in 1921 and operated until 1947. It was re-lit in 2002 and is now on the National Register of Historic Places.

upper manhattan

High Bridge Park

Forming the eastern border of Washington Heights is High Bridge Park. It was named after Manhattan's oldest standing bridge, which was built to carry the Croton Aqueduct into the city. Completed in 1848, the aqueduct carried over 35 million gallons of water a day from the Croton Reservoir, which is 40 miles north of the city. This historic bridge has been closed since 1970, but plans are in the works to restore and reopen it. During the 1970s, High Bridge Park was one of the most neglected in the city and had a large homeless population. During subsequent clean-ups, more than 250 tons of garbage were removed. While things have improved immensely, this is not a well-travelled part of Manhattan, so visiting after dark is not recommended.

 ### West 181st Street

If you venture west of Fort Washington Avenue, you'll discover a small but pleasant little restaurant district on West 181st Street.

 ### Saint Nicholas Avenue & West 181st Street

The main shopping area of northern Manhattan is concentrated along both Saint Nicholas Avenue and West 181st Street. Here you will find a large array of discount fashion, electronics, shoes, jewelry, and beauty supplies, along with many specialty shops.

George Washington Bridge

Towering over the Little Red Lighthouse is New York City's largest bridge, the George Washington. In the center of the span, the roadway is over 200 feet high, and the towers are over 600 feet. Opened in 1931, the bridge has the largest vehicular capacity of any bridge in the world, with 14 lanes of traffic. Over 100,000,000 vehicles cross the bridge annually. The original design called for the towers to be encased in white granite, but it was decided due to aesthetics (and cost) that the signature steel superstructure should remain exposed.

Did You Know?

On national holidays, the largest free-flying American flag in the world is suspended from the west tower of the George Washington Bridge. It is 90 feet long, 60 feet wide, and weighs over 450 pounds.

George Washington Bridge flag

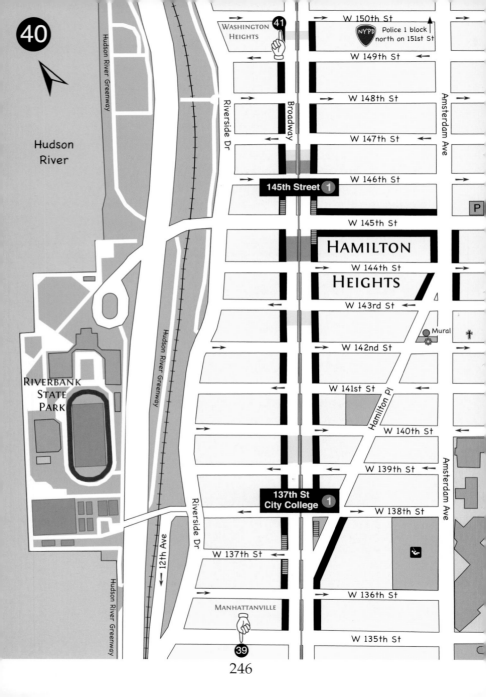

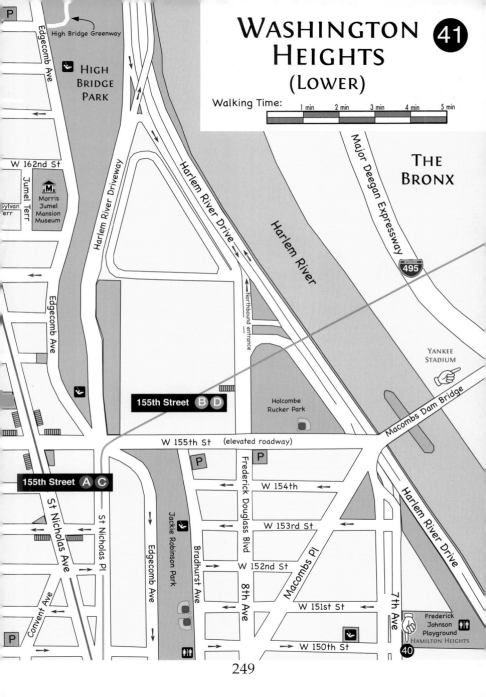

WASHINGTON
HEIGHTS
(LOWER)

41

Walking Time:

1 min   2 min   3 min   4 min   5 min

P

High Bridge Greenway

HIGH
BRIDGE
PARK

Edgecomb Ave

W 162nd St

Jumel Terr

Sylvan Terr

Morris
Jumel
Mansion
Museum

Harlem River Driveway

Harlem River Drive

Northbound entrance

Edgecomb Ave

155th Street **B** **D**

THE
BRONX

Major Deegan Expressway

Harlem River

495

YANKEE
STADIUM

Macombs Dam Bridge

Holcombe
Rucker Park

W 155th St   (elevated roadway)

155th Street **A** **C**

St Nicholas Ave

St Nicholas Pl

Jackie Robinson Park

Edgecomb Ave

Bradhurst Ave

Frederick Douglass Blvd

P

P

W 154th

W 153rd St

Macombs Pl

8th Ave

W 152nd St

W 151st St

Harlem River Drive

7th Ave

Frederick
Johnson
Playground
HAMILTON HEIGHTS

40

Convent Ave

P

W 150th St

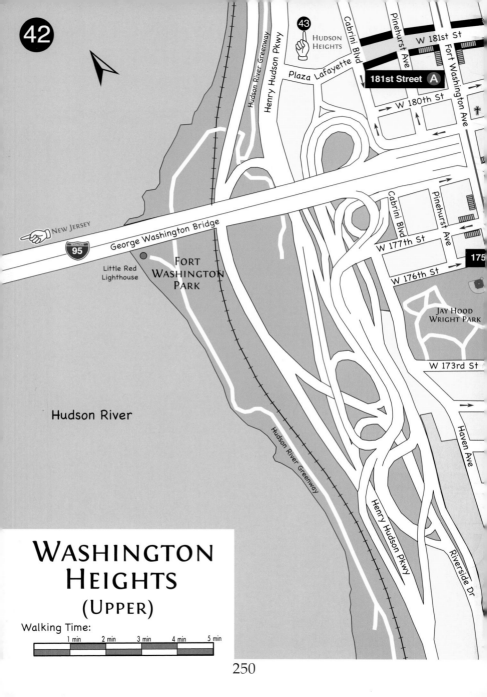

42

43
HUDSON
HEIGHTS

Hudson River Greenway

Henry Hudson Pkwy

Cabrini Blvd

Pinehurst Ave

Fort Washington Ave

W 181st St

Plaza Lafayette

181st Street A

W 180th St

Cabrini Blvd

Pinehurst Ave

NEW JERSEY

95 George Washington Bridge

W 177th St

175

W 176th St

Little Red
Lighthouse

FORT
WASHINGTON
PARK

JAY HOOD
WRIGHT PARK

W 173rd St

Hudson River

Haven Ave

Hudson River Greenway

Henry Hudson Pkwy

Riverside Dr

WASHINGTON
HEIGHTS
(UPPER)

Walking Time:

| 1 min | 2 min | 3 min | 4 min | 5 min |

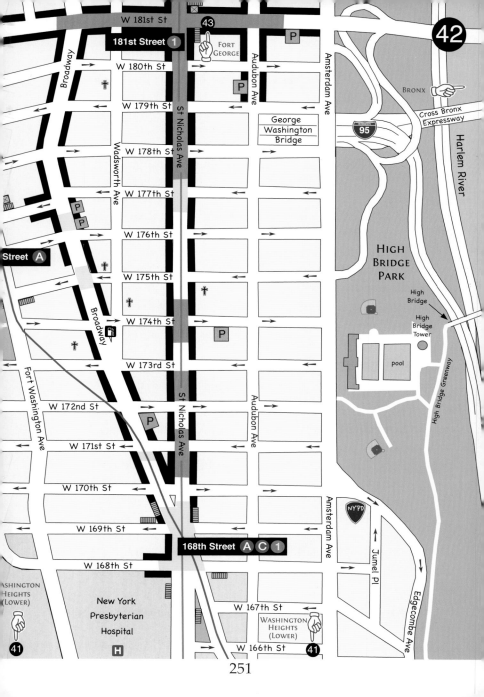

42

W 181st St

181st Street 1

FORT GEORGE

P

Broadway

W 180th St

Audubon Ave

P

Amsterdam Ave

BRONX

W 179th St

Cross Bronx
Expressway

George
Washington
Bridge

Wadsworth Ave

W 178th St

95

Harlem River

W 177th St

P

St Nicholas Ave

P

W 176th St

HIGH
BRIDGE
PARK

Street A

W 175th St

High
Bridge

W 174th St

High
Bridge
Tower

Broadway

P

W 173rd St

pool

High Bridge Greenway

W 172nd St

P

W 171st St

Fort Washington Ave

W 170th St

Audubon Ave

NYPD

W 169th St

Amsterdam Ave

Jumel Pl

168th Street A C 1

W 168th St

Edgecombe Ave

ASHINGTON
HEIGHTS
(LOWER)

New York
Presbyterian
Hospital

W 167th St

WASHINGTON
HEIGHTS
(LOWER)

41

H

41

W 166th St

HUDSON HEIGHTS
& FORT TRYON PARK
MAPS 43 & 44

Hudson Heights refers to the high ridge north of 181st Street and west of Broadway, overlooking the Hudson River. A quiet and affluent neighborhood, it has a distinctly different feel from the commercial district along Saint Nicholas Avenue, which is considered part of Washington Heights. Neighborhood boundaries are not as clear in this area, so you'll often hear of the area to the east of Fort Tryon Park called Fort Tryon or sometimes even "Fort George". This refers to the revolutionary era fort that once stood on Fort George hill near the east end of Dyckman Street.

M The Cloisters

The Cloisters is a branch of the Metropolitan Museum Of Art and houses their Medieval Collection. It was built in the 1930s and was designed to resemble a medieval abbey. Many original architectural details from European monasteries and churches were incorporated into the construction. While the collection is predominantly religious art from the 1200s – 1500s, the museum's most notable items are the original "Hunt Of The Unicorn" tapestries. In keeping with the theme, during the warmer months the museum features a garden of medieval herbs.

Bennet Park

This small park has the distinction of being the highest point in Manhattan at 265 feet above sea level.

 Fort Tryon Park

This 67-acre park dominates the landscape of the neighborhood. The home of the Cloisters Museum, the park also features hiking and walking paths, a restaurant, beautiful gardens, and many overlooks that provide grand views of the Hudson River, George Washington Bridge, and Upper Manhattan.

 West 187th Street

It's hard to believe you are still in Manhattan when you come upon this tiny main street and restaurant district in Hudson Heights along 187th Street.

 Dyckman Street

The main commercial thoroughfare of the Fort Tryon area is Dyckman Street, which is just to the north of the park. You'll find a vibrant restaurant district at the intersection of Dyckman and Broadway, dominated by interesting Spanish, Mexican, and fusion eateries.

upper manhattan

INWOOD   MAP 45

Inwood is the northernmost neighborhood on the island of Manhattan, and holds an important place in the city's history. A plaque in Inwood Park marks the site where the Dutch purchased Manhattan from the local Native American tribes in 1626. Inwood Hill Park also has the distinction of containing the only natural forest remaining in Manhattan. Formerly the site of a Lenape Indian village, artifacts and evidence of Native American habitation have been found throughout the area.

Baker Athletic Complex

At the very northern tip of Manhattan lies the Baker Athletic Complex. This 26-acre campus is part of Columbia University. Many athletic events take place throughout the year, the most popular being the Columbia Lions football games. Tickets are available by phone or online via the Columbia University website. If you look across Spuyten Duyvil Creek, you will see the famous Columbia "C" painted on the opposite cliffs. It was first painted by the Columbia rowing team in 1952, and has been maintained ever since.

Dyckman Farmhouse

The oldest farmhouse in Manhattan is located at the corner of Broadway and West 204th Street. It is now operated as the Dyckman House Museum.

 **West 207th Street**

Like much of northern Manhattan, Inwood is predominantly Hispanic, and has a bustling shopping and commercial district along 207th Street. It features discount shopping and many Spanish and Mexican-themed restaurants. A year-round farmers market can be found on Isham Street between Cooper and Seaman Streets on Saturday mornings.

Did You Know?

"Spuyten Duyvil" is Dutch for "Spouting Devil" and refers to the strong and dangerous tidal currents at Manhattan's northernmost tip, where Spuyten Duyvil Creek meets the Hudson River.

Restaurants along Dyckman Street

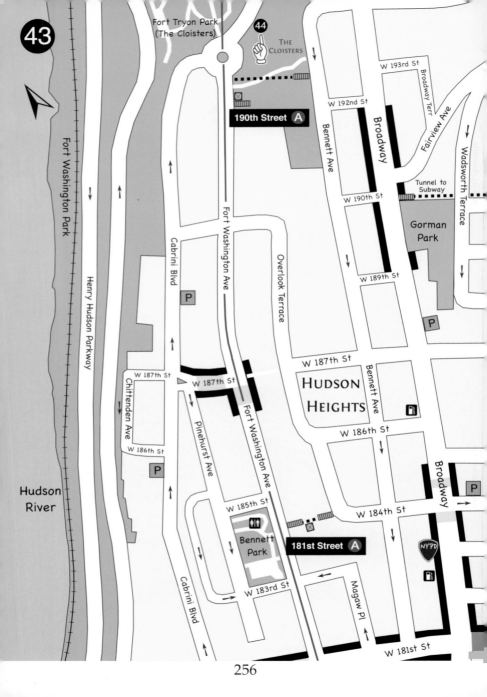

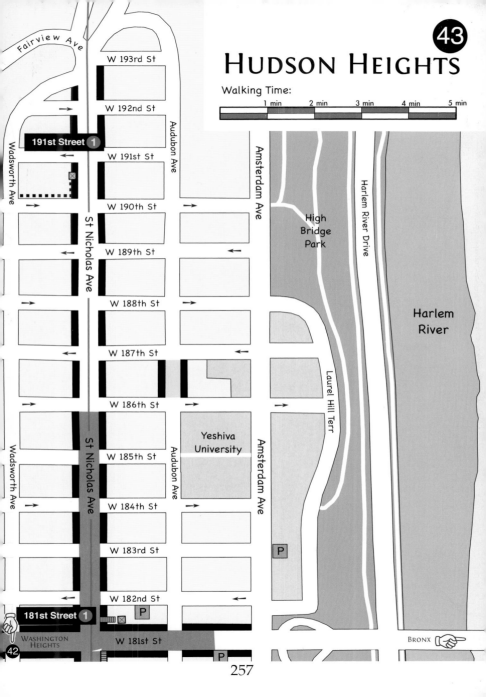

HUDSON HEIGHTS

Walking Time:

| | 1 min | 2 min | 3 min | 4 min | 5 min |

Fairview Ave

W 193rd St

W 192nd St

191st Street ①

W 191st St

Wadsworth Ave

St Nicholas Ave

Audubon Ave

W 190th St

W 189th St

W 188th St

W 187th St

W 186th St

W 185th St

W 184th St

W 183rd St

W 182nd St

Amsterdam Ave

High Bridge Park

Harlem River Drive

Harlem River

Laurel Hill Terr

Yeshiva University

Audubon Ave

Amsterdam Ave

P

181st Street ①

WASHINGTON HEIGHTS

P

W 181st St

P

BRONX

42

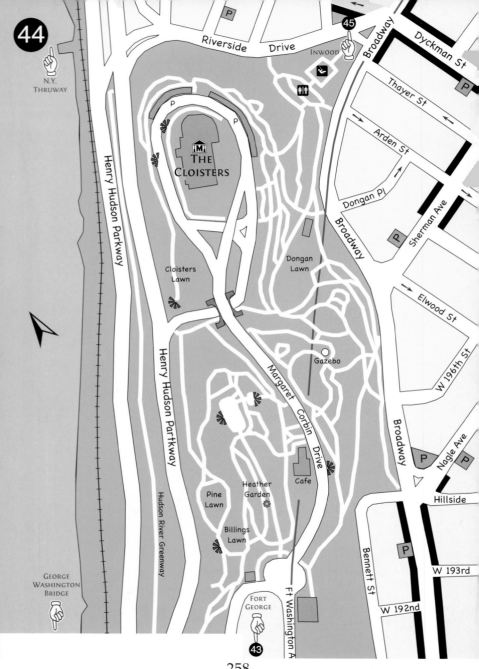

N.Y.
Thruway

Riverside   Drive

Inwood

P

45

Broadway

Dyckman St

P

Thayer St

Arden St

Dongan Pl

Broadway

Sherman Ave

P

Elwood St

W 196th St

P

P

P

Henry Hudson Parkway

The
Cloisters

Cloisters
Lawn

Dongan
Lawn

Gazebo

Margaret Corbin Drive

Hudson River Greenway

Heather
Garden

Cafe

Pine
Lawn

Billings
Lawn

Broadway

Nagle Ave

Hillside

Bennett St

W 193rd

W 192nd

George
Washington
Bridge

Fort
George

Ft Washington A

43

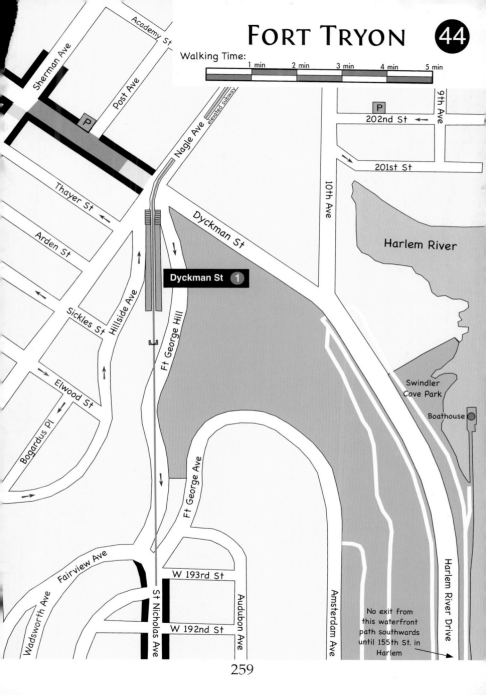

FORT TRYON

Walking Time:

1 min 2 min 3 min 4 min 5 min

Academy St

Sherman Ave

Post Ave

P

202nd St

P

9th Ave

201st St

Nagle Ave

elevated subway

10th Ave

Thayer St

Dyckman St

Harlem River

Arden St

Sickles St

Hillside Ave

Ft George Hill

Dyckman St ①

Elwood St

Bogardus Pl

Ft George Ave

Swindler Cove Park

Boathouse

Fairview Ave

Wadsworth Ave

St Nicholas Ave

W 193rd St

W 192nd St

Audubon Ave

Amsterdam Ave

Harlem River Drive

No exit from this waterfront path southwards until 155th St. in Harlem

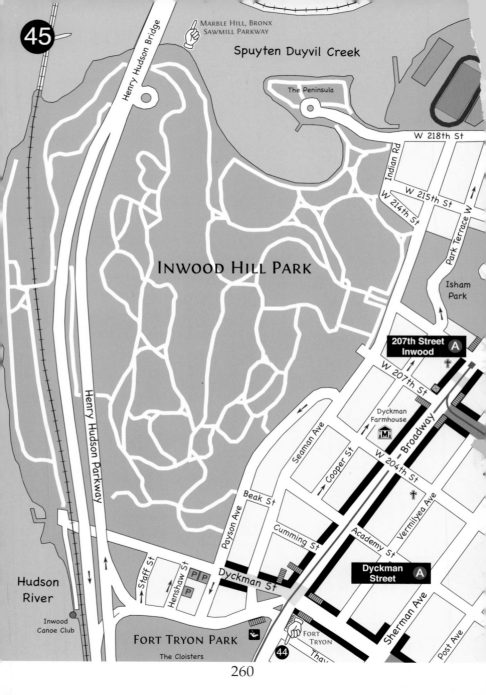

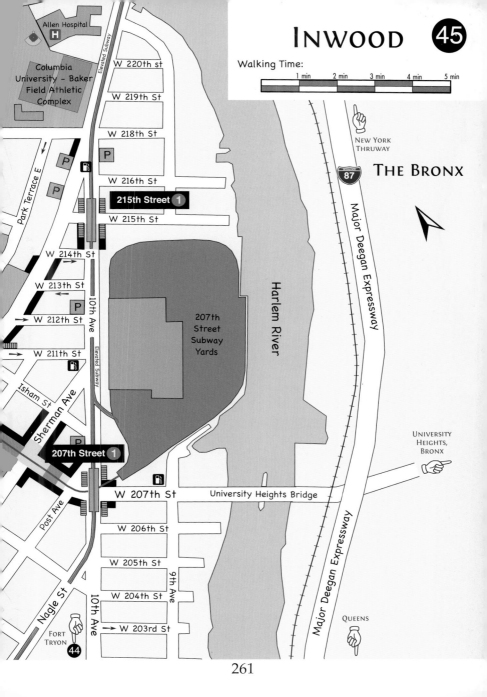

INWOOD 45

Walking Time:

| 1 min | 2 min | 3 min | 4 min | 5 min |

Allen Hospital

Columbia University - Baker Field Athletic Complex

W 220th St

W 219th St

W 218th St

W 216th St

215th Street ①

W 215th St

W 214th St

W 213th St

W 212th St

W 211th St

Park Terrace E

Elevated Subway

10th Ave

Elevated Subway

Isham St

Sherman Ave

207th Street ①

207th Street Subway Yards

Harlem River

NEW YORK THRUWAY

87

THE BRONX

Major Deegan Expressway

UNIVERSITY HEIGHTS, BRONX

W 207th St   University Heights Bridge

W 206th St

W 205th St

W 204th St

W 203rd St

Post Ave

Nagle St

9th Ave

10th Ave

Major Deegan Expressway

FORT TRYON

44

QUEENS

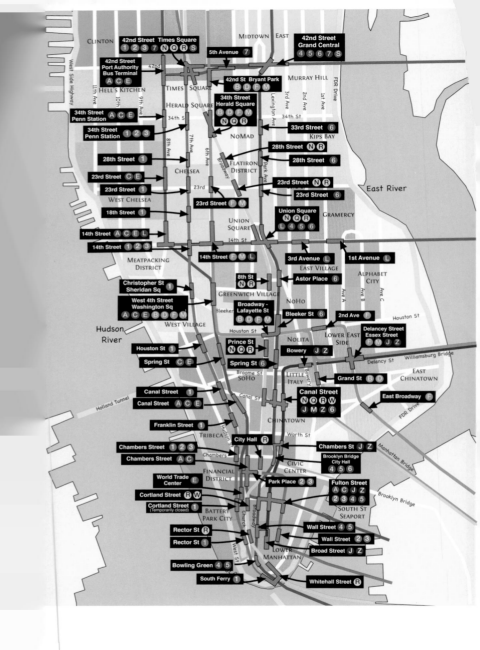

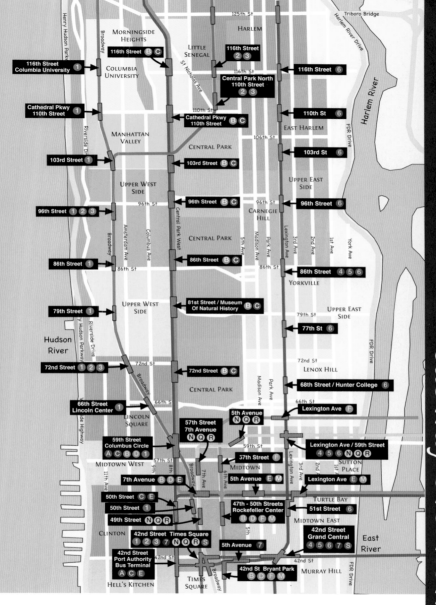

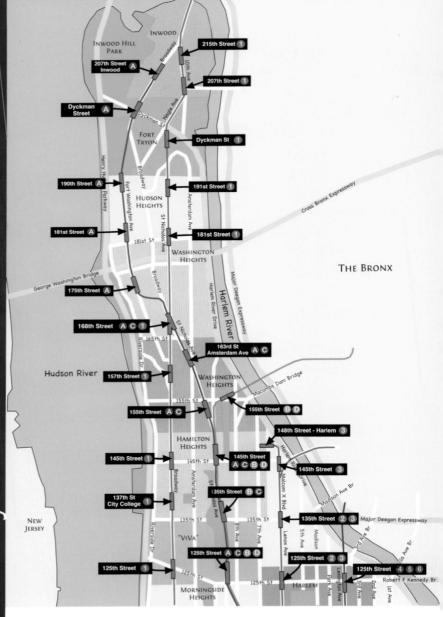

subway overview

While the New York City Subway we know today opened in October of 1904, the first subway in New York City was actually built by Alfred Ely Beach in 1870. It was a one-block, pneumatic "air-powered" subway that was constructed beneath Broadway between Murray and Warren Streets and operated for several years as a curiosity. The line's one and only station was lavishly decorated with chandeliers, a fountain, and a grand piano. Unfortunately, Beach ran into political and financial opposition and his plans of extending the line to Central Park never came to fruition. The tunnel was sealed and forgotten for decades until 1912, when workers discovered it during the construction of the Broadway line (the present-day "R" line). They were surprised by the ornate decorations and Beach's subway car still on the tracks. No trace of the tunnel remains today, but a plaque commemorating New York's very first subway can be found in its former location, which is now the City Hall station on the "R" line.

Beneath City Hall Park is another one of New York's subway secrets - the abandoned City Hall Station on the "6" line. This beautiful Beaux-Arts style station features mosaic tiled arches, skylights, and brass chandeliers. It was rendered obsolete when the city began running longer trains in the 1940s. The station can be seen if you stay on the downtown "6" train while it goes through the turn-around loop after the Brooklyn Bridge station.

subway overview

Getting Around

DRIVING & PARKING

The best advice I can give you is to not bring a car into Manhattan unless you really have to. If you do decide to drive, be prepared to pay for a parking garage. Many garages offer online coupons, and this is worth looking into. It can mean the difference between paying $15 or $50 for parking. In any case, be sure to read the parking rates carefully and check with the attendant if you have any questions. There is always a chance you might find street parking, but I'm going to be straight with you - it's unlikely. If you do find a spot on the street, check the parking regulation signs, then check them again. Make sure you haven't parked by a yellow curb, a driveway, or a fire hydrant. And that means ANY fire hydrant, even the ones that look like they haven't been in service since the 1950s.) Failure to take all these things into consideration will result in having your car towed. Trust me, you don't want this to happen. By the time you find your car, pay the $185 (minimum) towing fees and fines, you'll be wishing you had parked in a garage or better still, took mass transit into the city. In any case, if you do get towed in Manhattan, you will find your car at the tow pound on Pier 76 at West 38th Street and 12th Avenue. If you need to confirm your car is there, call 311.

TAXICABS

Hailing a taxi in New York City is simple. If a cab is empty and on duty, the white numbers on its roof will be illuminated. Stand at the curb and raise your arm, and the taxi will pull over to pick you up. Up to four people can legally ride in a New York taxi - three in the back, one in the front. Fares are calculated by a meter which is in plain sight on the dashboard. You can pay for your fare using cash or credit/debit cards.

Taxis are required by law to take passengers anywhere they wish

Taxi Fares

Initial fare	$2.50
Each 1/5 mile (about 4 blocks)	$0.40
Each minute in stopped traffic	$0.40
Peak rush hour surcharge	$1.00 (4pm - 8pm Mon - Fri)
Night surcharge	$1.00 (8pm - 6am)
New York State tax	$0.50
Flat fare to JFK Airport	$45.00
Tolls	

There is no charge for luggage or additional passengers

(For the most updated information on rates, see the Taxi and Limousine Commission's page on www.nyc.gov.)

to go in the five boroughs by the shortest possible route. All tolls must be paid by the passenger. At the end of the trip, it is customary to tip the driver between 15 and 20%. If you ever have a problem with a New York City taxi, note the medallion number and call 311.

BUSES

While the subway is the fastest way around town, New York City buses are quite useful in getting to and from areas of the city that do not have convenient subway service. An added benefit is the opportunity to sightsee on the way to wherever you're going; the downside is that you are at the mercy of the traffic.

Bus fare is $2.50, and can be paid with exact change (no bills) or a Metrocard, which is the preferred method and can be purchased at any subway station. If you pay with your Metrocard you can transfer free between intersecting bus and subway routes within two hours of paying your fare. If you pay with coins, ask the driver for a transfer card when you enter the bus, but be aware that this only allows a transfer to another bus.

Buses stop at designated bus stops which are marked by the route number. In most cases there is a route map attached to the signpost. All buses have destination signs on the front. Enter the bus by the front door and swipe your Metrocard. Buses stop every couple blocks, but pressing the yellow tape strips located between the windows or stop buttons found on grab bars will signal the driver to stop. Use the rear door to exit the bus.

More information and complete bus route maps can be found at web.mta.info/maps.

SUBWAY

The New York Subway was opened in 1904, and has been running 24 hours a day, 365 days a year ever since. The largest subway system in the world, it serves 468 stations and carries over 5 million riders each day. While some may remember the neglected stations and graffiti-covered trains of the 1970s and 80s, today the New York Subway system is clean, modern, and safe. The stations are well-maintained with easy-to-read signage. It is definitely the fastest and most efficient way of getting around the city.

Fares are $2.50 and are paid with a Metrocard, which can be purchased from vending machines or at the station booth. If you are not sure where you are going, free maps of the New York Subway are available from the station agent. Once you've paid your $2.50 fare and are in the subway system, you can ride as far as you want, and transfer to connecting trains for free. To enter, swipe your card at the turnstile, go through, and follow signs to the correct train. There are signs above each track informing you which trains stop there and the direction they are going. In Manhattan, tracks are typically designated as "uptown" or "downtown". The final destination of the train may also be on the sign such as - "Downtown and Brooklyn" or "Uptown and the Bronx". Trains run every few minutes during the day and become less frequent (every 20 minutes) after midnight.

Every station has an "Off Hours Waiting Area" which is designated by a yellow sign hanging from the ceiling. These are areas where the station agent can see you, and there are often security cameras in the vicinity. This is always a good place to wait for the train if you are alone, it's late, or the station is empty.

Stay away from the edge of the platform when the train arrives at the station and be sure to take note of the route number or letter which can be found on the front and side of the train. Allow exiting passengers to get off the train before you get on.

If the train is crowded and you don't get a seat, hold on to the overhead railings or poles in the center of the car. Nobody wants you falling on them when the train starts or stops. Don't place bags or packages on seats even if the train is empty. The NYC Transit police will give you an expensive ticket.

Inside each subway car is a route map and a system map. The conductor will make announcements for each upcoming station and which transfers are available there, as well as remind you what kind of train you are on and where it's going. Again, if its late or you are traveling alone, you may feel more comfortable riding in the car with the conductor. This is usually in the center of the train, and tends to stop right at the "Off Hours Waiting Area".

The subway can be a crowded place during rush hour. Mind your manners and be polite. Say "please" and "excuse me". Don't be afraid to ask for directions. While New Yorkers may have a reputation for being impatient and unfriendly, most will be quite happy to point you in the right direction if you're lost.

For more information go to http://new.mta.info.

getting around nyc

Index

Jim Schmitt has been exploring New York City for over three decades and has written several cartography-based books. He works in the fragrance industry as a perfumer by day, and by night can often be found in the New York Subway playing music on the guitar or mandolin. He has released two CDs of original music which are available on iTunes. For more information, visit www.jimschmitt.com

Visit www.knowingwhereyouregoing.com for neighborhood tour videos, updated maps and more.

A portion of the proceeds from the sale of this book will be donated to charities to aid the homeless in New York City.

about the author

Notes